DISCIPLING
THE BROTHER

*Congregational Discipline According
to the Gospel*

Marlin Jeschke

HERALD PRESS
Scottdale, Pennsylvania
Kitchener, Ontario

PREFACE

The recovery of authentic Christian community is the concern of a growing number of Christians today. The concern expresses itself in new experiments in congregational worship, K-groups, and even house churches. There is one dimension in authentic Christian community we dare not overlook. It is mutual aid in the path of discipleship.

Not much has been written on the subject of church discipline in the recent past. This is not a boast. It is a lament. With so little done in the field recently, this book can only propose to be a renewed beginning on the subject.

The reason so little has been published on church discipline is, of course, lack of interest in it. It is not only that publishers often reach for material of a more sensational nature which promises better financial return. Publishing is after all more or less a barometer of public interest. Theologians and the Christian laity too, unfortunately, have not considered this subject worth their time.

Now this situation might be understandable on the general Protestant scene, but it is surprising that discipline has received so little attention in the Anabaptist Mennonite tradition as well — this in spite of the fact that discipline is the second of seven articles in the Schleitheim Confession and is treated in just about every confession since. Compare this with the attention given to evangelism, relief, pacifism, the ministry, baptism, nonconformity, and similar topics. Church discipline seems to have become a theological blind spot.

There may be reasons for this. Quite often in the recent past Mennonite conferences and congregations have made serious mistakes in their attempts at church discipline, with the result that they now hesitate to engage in any discipline whatever. Also, quite frankly, the rank individualism of our society has crept into our churches. And so a kind of paralysis afflicts our congregations. We feel we should do something, but we don't quite know how to begin.

A neglect of discipline in the Anabaptist-Mennonite tradition would be most unfortunate because the motif of discipleship, which is central in this tradition, is the best possible basis for a doctrine of church discipline. As this book stresses, church discipline is the task of discipling the faltering brother in the church. This offers the possibility of moving beyond the legalism and "cheap grace" alternatives that have too often been the bane of Protestantism. Discipleship suggests something more than the formal "status" of justification as popularly conceived. At the same time it forestalls legalism by continually directing the Christian to the message and Spirit of Jesus rather than to church rules.

Furthermore, discipleship as a lifelong calling offers the possibility of moving beyond the popular notions of justification and sanctification. Too often a gap is put between justification and sanctification which distorts them both, so that a person's initial salvation is considered an easy absolution and his continued Christian life legalistic obedience — again the false alternatives of traditional Protestantism. But if the Christian calling is all of one piece, as discipleship suggests, then it makes both justification and sanctification a serious and genuine acceptance of the rule of God as defined in the gospel.

This book is an attempt to redeem the practice of church discipline by going back to the classical text on the subject, Matthew 18:15-18, and interpreting that text in the light of its setting — Jesus discipling His followers. If we can take what Jesus did with this discipleship community as the model of church discipline, we will have a sound beginning in the recovery of authentic Christian community today.

INTRODUCTION

Western Christianity has been suffering for a long time, and in various ways, from the relativizing impact of understandings of "tolerance" or of "humility" or "flexibility" which tended to dissolve the very possibility of common commitment in the believing community. This leads to the evident, if superficial, disadvantage that the church as a social organism, both locally and more broadly, is hamstrung by internal indecision. More profound is the loss of bindingness in her message and her morality. The democratic pluralism of the civil order is transposed paradoxically into the order of faith, as if there could be such a thing as faith where all views and all kinds of behavior are equally tolerable.

Marlin Jeschke is by far not the first to call for a recovery of discipline as the only hope of Christianity in a post-Christendom world. Even non-believing social scientists have said this about the Christian movement. But what this book does is far more than to identify a need; it discerns that the response to the need is not simply a stiffening of law, a reinforcement of authority, or a cooling of dissent, but rather an aspect — albeit little-recognized as such — of the grace of the gospel. The discipline — which he proposes to call "discipling" in order to underline its commonality with evangelism and baptism — is the renewal of the call to forgiveness, rendered real by the word of the brother. In numerous ways, from varied perspectives throughout the book, this is Jeschke's repeated point. Discipline is not to be held in tension or in balance with grace and forgiveness, it *is* grace and forgiveness. It is not rigor, regrettably necessary in structured communities but needing to be tempered with gentleness; it is gentleness at work (as the apostle says in so many words in Galatians 6:2).

We can thus leave for second place the preoccupation (correct enough in that second place) for more "character" or "decisiveness" or "effectiveness" in the mobilization of the church as a group of people with one mind and a concerted impact: in first place is the recovery of the forgiving love which can stand to address and restore the erring one because of the awareness of having oneself been thus addressed and restored by Christ Himself.

John H. Yoder, President
Goshen Biblical Seminary
Elkhart, Indiana

March, 1972

CONTENTS

Discipling the Brother

1

CHURCH DISCIPLINE PAST AND PRESENT

The mention of church discipline evokes mixed feelings in the typical church member of today. On the one hand, he intuitively recognizes some need for it, because after all, the Bible teaches it, and without it the meaning of church membership is soon canceled out. On the other hand, he has too many bad memories of unloving acts of church discipline in the past, cases of authoritarian legalistic action by church leaders on issues that turned out to have no connection with spiritual life.

Too often, unfortunately, it is the negative attitude that prevails in the average church member's mind, so that if someone suggests a recovery of church discipline today his conditioned reflex is, "No, thanks." He is grateful that the inquisition and witch-hunting and similar ecclesiastical nightmares are a thing of the past. But this attitude may be a somewhat hasty reaction. It would be too bad if we made ourselves the victims of other people's past mistakes.

> To abandon discipline because it has sometimes been ill-administered is as unwarranted as it would be to abandon worship on the ground that it has sometimes been ill-conducted. The relaxation of discipline has often more absurd results than ever attended its excess.[1]

The answer to bad church discipline is good church discipline, not no church discipline.

How do we achieve the recovery of good church discipline? The first step is an honest reply to objections. We must begin our study by reviewing the history of church discipline in order to identify those misconceptions that still haunt the subject. Only then can we liberate the church from the paralyzing effects of ambivalent attitudes.

The Old Testament Background

Even if it may not be this week's fad in American theology, something in the nature of church discipline has always been part of the life of the people of God, since discipline has to do with the definition of existence in the community of faith. The roots of the idea reach back into the life of Israel in the Old Testament. In the earliest era of Israel there was a curse, often

14

though not exclusively employed in war, through which Israel's enemies were consecrated to the Lord in death, and the property of the enemy was likewise devoted to destruction. Examples of this are the destruction of Jericho and the killing of Agag by Samuel. Joshua 6:16-21; 1 Samuel 5:1-4, 32, 33.

Sometimes a member of Israel broke the faith and thereby fell under the curse. This happened to Achan when he defiled himself with something consecrated to destruction, according to Joshua 7. Because Israel was a theocratic community, the curse was primarily a religious ban and not merely capital punishment. Someone who in a fundamental sense violated the covenant forfeited membership in the community and was removed in order to preserve the holiness of the people.

When after the deportation and dispersion Israel no longer possessed political independence, but became a "church" with a synagogue pattern of life, the form of the curse changed from death to banishment. The outlines of the new form of discipline can be traced in Ezra. From this time onward to fall under the curse meant not to be killed, but to be banned and perhaps also to have one's property confiscated. "And thus began the practice, continued through the Christian centuries, of interdiction and excommunication."[2]

In the centuries following the time of Ezra discipline was developed and refined in the Jewish community. The system of discipline described in the Talmud, though it may never have operated rigidly and uniformly, ran thus. First and least severe was a rebuke or censure called a *nezifah*. This was employed usually in cases of disrespect for rabbinic authority. The *nezifah* was effective for one day according to the Babylonian Talmud, and for seven days according to the Palestinian Talmud. The person standing under this form of discipline was required to go to his home, refrain from business or entertainment, and not appear in the sight of the rabbi who had pronounced the rebuke over him.

Next there was an excommunication called a *niddui*. Often compared to what in the Middle Ages was termed minor excommunication, it was preceded by three warnings, and its pronouncement was always accompanied by the words, "May that man live in separation." Its duration according to the Babylonian Talmud was seven days, according to the Palestinian, thirty. The Talmud lists twenty-four offenses punishable by this excommunication, mostly insubordination to Mosaic law or its authoritative rabbinic interpretation and application.

The subject of this ban was required to don a mourning habit and to refrain from bathing or from cutting his hair or from wearing shoes or sandals. No one was to eat with him, and others were forbidden contact with him, except for his wife and children. He could not be counted in the ritual number necessary for prayers. If he died while under the ban, a stone was placed on his grave to indicate the fact, and his relatives were forbidden to rend their garments or to engage in the customary practices of mourning.

An individual who remained incorrigible after the expiration of three *nidduis* fell under the *cherem*, the curse. According to one authority this curse could be imposed only in the presence of ten members of the community — that is, the minimum complement needed to comprise a synagogue.[3] It was at this ban that sometimes lights were extinguished and a symbolic bier carried out of the house as in a funeral rite, indicating that the subject of the ban was considered dead, cut off from Israel and from Israel's spiritual life. Serious as this ban was, it was not irrevocable. When the individual reformed, the ban could be revoked by the proper authorities.[4]

Discipline in the New Testament

The conception of church discipline in the New Testament clearly comes out of Judaism. The teaching attributed to Jesus in Matthew 18 bears marked similarities to a passage in the Testament of the Twelve Patriarchs, Gad 6:3, 7.

> Love ye one another from the heart; and if a man sin against thee, speak peaceably to him, and in thy soul hold not guile; and if he repent and confess, forgive him. . . . And if he be

> shameless and persist in his wrong-doing, even so
> forgive him from the heart, and leave to God the
> avenging.[5]

Also the instruction to treat an unresponsive sinner as a Gentile and tax collector has for its background the excommunication practice of the Palestinian Jewish community during the time of Jesus. Like Judaism, the primitive church had a strong sense of identity as a community in distinction from the world, and its expectation was a life radically different from that of the world.

The origin of church discipline in Judaism should not, however, blind us to the difference between it and Jewish discipline. The church recalled, for example, the contrast between the Jewish leaders and Jesus in their respective treatments of the woman taken in adultery. John 8:1-12. Also one should note the discipline Paul first exercised as an orthodox Pharisee and later received as a Christian from the orthodox community, contrasting it with his practice as a Christian apostle. Remember that Paul never broke with Judaism, but remained all his life under the discipline of the synagogue. The difference between the Christian and Jewish disciplines lay essentially in the Christian rejection of coercion and violence as a means of establishing the righteous community under God. The parable of the wheat and the tares is decisive on this point.

The outlines of church discipline in the New Testament Christian movement are not hard to sketch. There is the classic text in Matthew 18:15-18 and its parallel in Luke 17:3 about admonishing a sinning brother and, if he repents, forgiving him, or if he does not, considering him a Gentile or tax collector. The Book of Acts shows instances of discipline in the early Christian community (the case of Ananias and Sapphira, for example). In Romans 16:17 Paul advises avoidance of those who cause dissension. In 1 Corinthians 5 he explicitly directs the excommunication of a recalcitrant offender, and in 2 Corinthians 2:5-9 he encourages the readmission of an excommunicated person. In Galatians 6:1 he asks those who are spiritual to restore someone overtaken in a trespass. Finally the pastoral letters contain several references to avoidance of the disobedient, hypocrites, and factious. 2 Thessalonians 3:6, 14; 2 Timothy 3:2-5; Titus 3:10.

We will not go into a systematic discussion here of the nature of discipline according to the New Testament, because that is the substance of the chapters which follow. There each important passage mentioned above will at some point come under study. Formulating a theology of discipline from the New Testament means something more, however, than shuffling the pertinent texts and arranging them into a handbook. Such an approach may seem useful for pastoral purposes, but it does not provide an adequate theological foundation. Too often it makes the New Testament an instrument of denominational polity or a collection of proof texts for theories brought to it from elsewhere. Too often, also, discipline is considered an assortment of rules and policies to be used for a similar assortment of moral contingencies — a scheme for "codifying sins and tariffing sentences."[6] What is needed is a vision of discipline within the framework of Christian faith as a whole. It must be seen as rooted in the very foundation of the church's life, which is the good news of the coming of the reign of God.

A few scholars surprisingly venture the claim that discipline — or at least an aspect of it such as excommunication — was unknown in the church of New Testament times. They reach such conclusions through the dubious method of first defining discipline from practices in the Middle Ages or Reformation times and then arguing that they cannot find such discipline in the pages of the New Testament.

Now admittedly "discipline" is not a New Testament word, though it derives from the same root as the word "disciple." Nevertheless it may be useful to be reminded that the term "discipline" is not found in the New Testament, for that cautions us not to impose upon it ideas from later periods of history, but to give meaning to the word and to structure our faith and practice according to the New Testament itself. We take the position that the gospel is our authority for faith and practice.

The Development of Penance

With regard to the development of church discipline in the history of Christendom, one historian thinks it striking

> how in the sparse literature which has appeared concerning the office of the keys and church discipline, again and again writers hurriedly turn from the New Testament to the Reformers. In this way their orientation is determined by an attitude toward Rome.[7]

The comment advises us not to overlook the intervening era, which has much indeed to teach us, negatively as well as positively.

In the post-apostolic period through the first two or three centuries discipline was a prominent concern of the church, as is indicated by the debate over the possibility of forgiveness for post-baptismal sin and the formation of categories of mortal sins. It was made more acute through the problems raised by the persecutions in the third century — how to deal with those of the lapsed (persons who had denied the faith under persecution) who were apparently genuinely penitent. The central issue in this era was whether excommunicated persons could be reinstated in the church, and if so under what conditions.

The penitential system appears to have developed gradually during the second century. In the Apostolic Constitutions, a treatise of A.D. 252-270 from Syria,[8] there is a description of an early stage of the emerging penitential system. In these constitutions the bishop is instructed thus:

> When you see the offender in the congregation, you are to take the matter heavily, and to give orders that he be expelled from it. Upon his expulsion, the Deacons are likewise to express their concern, to follow and to find the party, and to detain him for awhile without the Church. In a little time they are to come back, and to intercede with you on his behalf, in like manner as our Saviour interceded with His Father for sinners, saying, as we learn from the Gospel, "Father, forgive them; for they know not what they do." Then you shall order him to be brought into the Church; and after having examined whether he be truly penitent, and fit to be re-admitted into full Communion, you shall direct him to continue in a state of mortification for the space of two, three, five, or seven weeks, according to the nature of the offense; and then, after some proper admonitions, shall dismiss [or absolve] him.[9]

A person under penance engaged in dramatic acts of remorse in evidence of genuine repentance — sackcloth and ashes, weeping at the door of the church, and interceding with the elders for readmission — until the bishop restored him.

It should be observed that there were no

grades of penitents here yet and that the duration of penance was still relatively brief. Also the Canons of Elvira (around A.D. 305) mention no penitential stations.[10] But by the fourth century there were three or four stations of penance through which excommunicated penitents passed. These were part of the rigorous system usually associated with the church order of this era. First the offender was excommunicated for mortal sin. Then he made confession to a presbyter who admitted him to penance and assigned the forms of public penance through which he was to pass (the stations of hearer, kneeler, and stander). Finally the penitent was absolved by the bishop in a public liturgy preceding Easter Communion. The Council of Ancyra in Galatia in A.D. 314 "alludes to these stations as 'the defined grades.' The system is an accepted system; and is acquiring a technical terminology."[11]

At this time also the duration of penance came to be fixed. According to Basil, bishop of Caesarea in the middle of the fourth century, such persons as were guilty of, for example, incontinence, were for the first year

> excluded entirely from the whole service, and were to stand weeping at the church door, which was the Station of mourners; in the year following, they were admitted to that of hearers; in the third to that of the Prostrate, called [properly] the penance; in the fourth they were permitted to stand with the faithful whilst they communicated, but might not themselves partake with

them. And this I have termed the Station of *consistentes* or "by-standers"; and thus, at last, they were restored in full to all their privileges, and were allowed to communicate.[12]

Although the terms of penance were spelled out in detail, they varied according to the different canonical books, and the terms tended to grow more severe even while (and perhaps because) their effectiveness diminished, especially in the Eastern part of the church. "At the same time, and by the very same degrees, wherein the efficacy and power of [discipline] declined, the forms and show of it increased and multiplied."[13] One historian remarks, "Not till the end of the third century was a rigorous and fixed system of penitential discipline established, and then this could hardly maintain itself a century."[14] Still another historian says, in summary, "It would appear that the practice of public penance nowhere died out, but that it ceased to be the practice of the main stream of offending Christians."[15]

When we review the history of this era, what do we discover to be the main features of its discipline? For one thing, sin was taken very seriously, although the church's focus seems to have been restricted to the three cardinal sins — murder, unchastity, and idolatry. For another thing, there was a strong sense of the distinction between the church and the world, in the light of which excommunication and penance carried a good deal of force. Unfortunately there is little mention of admonition within the Christian community in this era or of attempts to save offenders by means of preventive counsel.

The Advent of Celtic Penance

In the later Middle Ages the meaning and structure of disciplinary practice shifted in a major way through the influence of a system of confession that arose in British Christianity. In the words of the historian Watkins:

> It is one of the most remarkable facts of Church history that never at any time did the continental system of public penance gain a foothold in these [British] islands. . . . They had an important monastic system with many peculiar features, and in connexion with this monastic system they developed a procedure of Penance, which not only held the field as regards the British Isles, but was destined to meet and to supersede the existing penitential procedure of the continent.[16]

Sometimes called the Celtic penitential system, this penance originated in the vigorous spiritual life of the early Irish monasteries, where monks voluntarily confessed their sins and problems to each other in order to receive forgiveness and spiritual counsel.

The Celtic penitential system was considerably

different from the earlier Latin one. Whereas the Latin penitential discipline was the method for a person to regain entrance into the church after having been excommunicated for post-baptismal sin, and was a public penance, unrepeatable (at least till the Third Council of Toledo, A.D. 389[17]), the Celtic penitential was a periodic private confession within the monastic community or, as later adapted to the parish system, to a parish priest. Not only the confession but also the penance imposed (fasting, prayers, alms, even pilgrimages) was not necessarily public, nor did it require appearance at public worship, for the absolution too was not spoken in a public liturgy by the bishop but in private by the priest. Moreover, absolution came eventually to be pronounced before the satisfaction of penance instead of after. The Latin penance was one to be avoided, since it signified the shame of a fall and of excommunication. The Celtic was one to be sought, since it signified the virtue of piety and forestalled excommunication.

The Celtic system came to the continent under Charles the Great through the British scholars he brought to his court, and it is not surprising that this system in due time prevailed throughout the Catholic Church, on the continent as well as in Britain. At the Council of Chalon, held sometime between A.D. 639 and 654, the bishops present expressed the judgment that "the Penance of sinners . . . we deem to be useful for all men."[18] In the Dialogue of Egbert, Archbishop of York from 732 to 736, it was already a custom considered to carry the force of law for laymen as well as clergy to betake themselves to confessors annually in the twelve days before Christmas. Mandatory annual confession eventually became canon law at the Fourth Lateran Council in 1215, which decreed:

> Every fidelis of either sex shall after the attainment of years of discretion confess his sins with all fidelity to his own priest at least once in the year. Otherwise let him during life be repelled from entering the Church and when dead let him lack Christian burial.[19]

Actually the change in penitential practice of which we are speaking was not simply a replacement of the Latin system by the Celtic, for to some extent and for some time the two coexisted in the church. One historian observes that according to the capitularies of the Frankish kings, after the seventh century a provision was made that

> if anyone had made a private and voluntary confession, he should do penance in private, while if he had made a public and open confession, he should also openly before the Church do penance in accordance with the canonical grades of penance.[20]

The two systems did not, however, simply

continue to coexist. "Public penance gradually grew rare and came to be known as solemn penance," imposed only for notorious and scandalous crimes.[21] Also, as the decree of the Fourth Lateran Council quoted above shows, failure to comply with the new requirement of repeatedly making private confession led to excommunication. So the Celtic and old Latin systems in effect stratified into the small and great ban and became grades of severity in the church's evolving system of discipline.

In the final analysis the most significant development in this era was the confusion between the church and the world that came into being with the Constantinian era. Since citizenship in the state was integrated with membership in the church, discipline became integrated with secular law, as can be seen from the claim of Sixtus IV in 1484 that absolutions in the confessional were binding upon secular courts. Thus the apparent gains from the introduction of the milder Celtic penitential system were just that — only apparent and not real. For excommunication under the early Latin penance had at least not meant loss of civil rights. It had depended only upon the moral power of the church.

Reformation Ventures

For the Reformers church discipline was, in

the words of one historian, "no incidental question."[22] Luther wrote one treatise on the power of the keys and another dealing with the problem caused by the breakdown of the unity and authority of the church and the resultant uncertainty over the validity of the ban. Nevertheless Luther never formally instituted an order for church discipline, even though, as one scholar asserts, "Only ignorance or thoughtlessness can claim that the motif of church discipline was foreign to Luther."[23] The first *Kirchenordnung* of Wittenberg in 1533 contains no church order for penance, confession, or the ban.

As late as 1540 Luther was tempted toward an organized venture, but it did not materialize, and he himself gives the reason: "I would gladly institute it, but it's not the time for it yet." The rationalization behind this statement is curious indeed: "If only there were people who would allow themselves to be disciplined!" But that was not the only reason, perhaps not even the chief one. For despite his hesitation to inaugurate a formal discipline, Luther did sporadically and almost recklessly practice it himself and called upon other Lutheran leaders to do likewise.[24]

What seems to have been a more important restraining influence was his fear of the Reformation church falling back into the evils of the Catholic ban. Luther had already rejected this ban with its physical penalties by 1537. Hence the ideal discipline emerging in the earliest

Lutheran tradition was an emphasis on the role of preaching, with exclusion from Communion as the final resort. "According to the evangelical Lutheran view the central point of church discipline is exclusion from the sacraments; discipline is above all a discipline of the Lord's Supper."[25]

Unfortunately Luther was not consistent with himself. On several occasions he advocated that an individual banned from the Lord's Supper who failed to respond to the ban be given over to the secular authorities and exiled. As his rejection of the Catholic ban shows, Luther saw the problems of such a relation of church and state, but while not desiring it theoretically, he nevertheless furthered it practically. At one time, for example, Luther stated that "church discipline would be superfluous if the state would be thorough enough in its law enforcement."[26]

It is not too surprising therefore that in the post-Reformation period discipline in Lutheran territory fell into the hands of the state by default precisely because Luther had refused to institute a definite church order for it. The consistory, an emergency organization growing out of the practice of visitation, became a permanent government-related organization already in the 1540's. Hence what came out of the Reformation on this score was just the opposite of what Luther intended in his original insight and position.

The eventual pattern was that a minister could exclude people from Communion, but beyond that the consistory reserved the right to excommunicate, impose fines, or otherwise punish offenders.[27] The resort to such measures was in effect a return to the great ban of the pre-Reformation church. However, with the advent of rationalism and the enlightenment practically all discipline ceased. In some parts of Germany the state even began specifically to forbid certain forms of discipline and to restrict the powers of the church.[28]

In contrast to Lutheran hesitancy in discipline the churches of the Reformed tradition in southern Germany and Switzerland boldly instituted it. Zwingli in his *Auslegung und Begründung der Schlussreden* devoted an entire article to the ban.

What is most notable about the system that developed under Zwingli is the church's intentional use of the secular authorities. For Zwingli the Christian magistrates functioned as elders within the church in the execution of discipline. He left the right of excommunication to magistrates, as the First and Second Helvetic Confessions point out. This state of affairs reflected Zwingli's theory: "The preaching office is the guiding spirit, the authorities *(die Obrigkeit)* the executive organ of the state church organism."[29] In 1525

a tribunal was created consisting of two secular

priests, two members of the larger council, and two members of the smaller council, but this institution was still far removed from an organization of the ecclesiastical congregation; it simply reported its findings to the secular authority.[30]

Of the major Reformers the systematic Calvin was the one who went farthest in the implementation of discipline. He devoted a chapter to discipline in the Fourth Book of the Institutes. In it he says:

> As the saving doctrine of Christ is the soul of the Church, so discipline forms the ligaments which connect the members together, and keep each in its proper place. Whoever, therefore, either desire the abolition of all discipline, or obstruct its restoration, whether they act from design or inadvertency, they certainly promote the entire dissolution of the Church. [31]

Calvin made acceptance of discipline a condition of his return to Geneva in 1541, and in his establishment of the consistory of twelve men, according to the *Ordonnances*, he insisted upon the church's independence of the civil authorities.

In actual fact this independence was not strictly maintained, for the magistrates were expected to supply political support for the church. In the Gallican Confession magistrates are said to be appointed by God to suppress crimes against the first as well as against the second table of the decalogue. Even when the independence of the church was maintained, the actual functioning of the consistory was in the nature of a deutero-government. The methods it employed, such as monetary fines for delinquency in attending church, were often inconsistent with the gospel.[32]

Discipline was also, of course, an important part of the Anabaptist movement. It was the second of seven articles treated in the Schleitheim Confession of 1527:

> We are agreed as follows on the ban: The ban shall be employed with all those who have given themselves to the Lord, to walk in His commandments, and with all those who are baptized into the one body of Christ and who are called brethren or sisters, and yet who slip sometimes and fall into error and sin, being inadvertently overtaken. The same shall be admonished twice in secret and the third time openly disciplined or banned according to the command of Christ. Matthew 18. But this shall be done according to the regulation of the Spirit before the breaking of bread, so that we may break and eat one bread, with one mind and in one love, and may drink of one cup.[33]

Discipline was taught and practiced by the Hutterites in Moravia, and in the Netherlands Menno Simons wrote three tracts on the subject.[34]

Because of their circumstances the Anabaptists did not — and because of their convictions they would not — use political power in the exercise of discipline, although later some Mennonite colonies of South Russia did. Of note is the fact that the Netherlands Anabaptists engaged in the

33

practice of shunning for some decades. Then when this practice had about run its course in Dutch Mennonitism it was taken over by the Amish, followers of Jacob Amman, who use various forms of it to this day. Shunning was one of the issues in the schism between the Amish and Swiss Brethren in the 1690's. Partly under the influence of the Anabaptist movement the Church of the Brethren also taught and practiced discipline from the time of its founding under Alexander Mack.[35]

In the English-speaking world it was in Scotch Presbyterianism and Puritanism that "the rigorous discipline of Geneva found its most genial soil."[36] The Scottish Church continued the policy of requesting state support begun by the Reformed Church on the continent. According to the seventeenth-century Scottish divines, "It is [the Christian magistrate's] most solemn duty to support the ministry in its exercise of the 'key of discipline,' by every lawful means in his power."[37]

Puritanism in England did not, fortunately, have the political position to use this arrangement, whether it wanted to or not, and for that reason perhaps fashioned a doctrine of church discipline independent of secular authorities. The Puritan confession of 1589 sets forth its view of discipline virtually as a paraphrase of Matthew 18. Understandably the authority of the whole congregation is emphasized and that of the clergy correspondingly limited. Popular opinion often brands the Puritans as legalists, but what strikes the impartial reader is their concern to follow, in their "watch and care," the directives of the New Testament.[38]

As is known, Methodism from the outset possessed a vigorous discipline. The societies must be commended for the primary emphasis they gave to positive spiritual counsel, which resulted in the sanctified lives of their members. At the same time they also, and very properly, had recourse where necessary to negative measures. But it is here that an ambiguity arises in Methodist discipline by virtue of its relation to Anglicanism. For those who were expelled from the societies fell back into the broad bosom of the Anglican Church, with which Wesley always remained connected. This inevitably suggested that the disciplined life of the societies was not in the end really normative but rather a counsel of perfection, somewhat as in the pre-Reformation church. When Methodism later became an independent communion, Wesleyan practice was of course translated into church discipline.[39]

It is not possible to follow the history of our subject beyond the shores of Europe except in a very general way. The most important development that has taken place in the modern chapter of the story is the separation of church and state, a development that the perspective of time may show to be as epochal as Constantine or as the

Reformation. As is well known, a free-church situation exists in nearly every non-European part of the world, where so-called "mission churches" or "younger churches" often find themselves in the position of the primitive church. A recent edition of an encyclopedia of religion devotes a whole section to the discussion of discipline in the younger churches.[40] A German author affirms it a necessity in the missionary setting,[41] and so does Lesslie Newbigin, a bishop in the church of South India: "The Church in a non-Christian cultural environment has to take seriously the business of discipline . . . because without this the Church's witness to the non-Christian world becomes hopelessly compromised."[42]

The Contemporary Situation

If much of the church is in a position similar to that of early Christianity, then in a sense we have come full circle in the history of discipline. In that light the one remarkable fact about discipline today is the apparent loss of interest in the subject, at least in comparison with the concern it received in the early church. Numerous nineteenth-century books on the doctrine of the church still discuss discipline in some fashion — for example, as one of the "powers of the church." It is striking, however, that in the spate of books on the doctrine of the church coming out of the ecumenical movement and the rise of biblical theology since the second World War there is scant treatment of discipline. While most of these books discuss the meaning of the holiness of the church, few specifically mention discipline as a way of dealing with sin in the church.

Nevertheless there are some voices calling for the recovery of a sound and biblical discipline. Emil Brunner says:

> The function of Church discipline has . . . to a very great extent, fallen into disuse. . . . The Church ought to know, however, that this absence of any kind of Church discipline inevitably gives the impression that to belong or not to belong to the Church comes to the same thing in the end, and makes no difference in practical life. . . . [43]

A Lutheran theologian says:

> Of all the problems that press upon the church today and demand solution I know of none so theologically complicated, and thus none whose solution is so urgent and of such a fundamental and far-reaching significance, as the problem of church discipline. [44]

A British writer says:

> [Today] discipline, with its suggestions of hardness and rigidity, is contrasted unfavorably with the New Testament emphasis on love and the Spirit of Christ. But the plain fact is that our Christian life has been impoverished as the result of this lack of proper discipline . . . so that instead of helping each other to "grow in grace and

in the knowledge of our Lord Jesus Christ," we have been, albeit unconsciously, holding each other back.[45]

We could add to these quotes others from the Presbyterian, Methodist, United Church of Christ, and Southern Baptist traditions as well as from the Mennonite Church.[46] This broad spectrum shows that concern for discipline is not necessarily the preoccupation of sectarianism. These are responsible voices calling for the reexamination of the subject and the implementation in church life of whatever such reexamination demands. This sense of urgency is shared by many ministers and laymen today who feel that the church should be able to do something about Christians whose lives are threatened with spiritual shipwreck, something beyond condemnation or apathy, but church traditions and public opinion being what they are, these concerned ministers and laymen are at a loss.

If concern about church discipline is not a preoccupation of sectarians, but is shared by many responsible people in the mainstream of Christianity, perhaps it is time to see discipline at the center of Christian faith. Church discipline is part of the gospel. It is an inescapable consequence of the discipling process we call the proclamation of the good news of the kingdom of God. Church discipline is the act of attempting to disciple a brother who is in danger

38

of abandoning the faith through any particular act or attitude. Such an act of discipling is the corollary of evangelism, which is the initial act of discipling.

This book is an attempt, therefore, to work toward an evangelical church discipline. It is not restricted to a study of church discipline in the New Testament, although the New Testament naturally must be taken into consideration. Neither is this a historical study, although we have just reviewed the doctrine and practice of the church in history and attempted to learn from this record. Again, this is not a denominational study or a comparative study of discipline in several denominational traditions. This is an attempt to set up a constructive model.

The discussion in this book limits the subject to exclude some practices often — and rightly — designated discipline, such as gathered worship, the study of Scripture, public and private prayer, and even fasting. These are not just good, they are indispensable in the Christian life and the life of the church. Corrective discipline must presuppose them. And yet in themselves they are not enough. The church can and must have recourse to corrective discipline where self-discipline breaks down, as special medical help often becomes necessary even though it usually assumes hygiene and the normal vitality of human life. There is room for a study on emergency care of souls, and isolating such a subject for special attention does not at all imply that we lose sight of other tasks of the church. On the contrary, it is the comprehensive view that enables us to recover a healthy practice of corrective church discipline.

Our procedure will be to take for an outline Matthew 18:15-18, which can rightly, I think, be regarded as the classical biblical text for church discipline. We shall examine this passage in the light of its context and of other relevant scriptural passages. We shall then attempt to portray systematically what discipline based on the gospel looks like — from beginning to end, from recognition of the problem to, if necessary, the excommunication and hopefully restoration of a Christian brother.

2

THE KEYS
OF THE KINGDOM
Mandate for Discipline

.

The basic New Testament text on church discipline is Matthew 18:15-18. It has always been considered important, partly no doubt because it represents the word of Christ, and partly because it offers systematic instruction upon the subject as a whole. Because of its importance, let me quote the passage here in full.

> If your brother sins against you, go and tell him his fault, between you and him alone. If he listens to you, you have gained your brother. But if he does not listen, take one or two others along with you, that every word may be confirmed by the evidence of two or three witnesses. If he refuses to listen to them, tell it to the church; and if he refuses to listen even to the church, let him be to you as a Gentile and a tax collector. Truly, I say to you, whatever you bind on earth shall be bound in heaven, and whatever you loose on earth shall be loosed in heaven.

Together with this passage we should examine Matthew 16:18, 19, where Jesus says, "You are Peter, and on this rock I will build my church. . . . I will give you the keys of the kingdom of heaven, and whatever you bind on earth shall be bound in heaven, and whatever you loose on earth shall be loosed in heaven." John 20:22, 23 is another related text. In that passage the risen Christ breathes upon the gathered disciples, saying, "Receive the Holy Spirit. If you forgive the sins of any, they are forgiven; if you retain the sins of any, they are retained." These texts have shared a long association in the history of interpretation and as a group have been the basis for the church's claim to the power of the keys. Do these passages provide a basis for church discipline? If so, what is the nature of the discipline they support?

The traditional medieval interpretation of the power of the keys was that the life of men in this world as well as their destiny in the next was subject to the will of ecclesiastical princes. The promise of Matthew 16:18, 19 and 18:15-18 that what was bound or loosed on earth would be bound or loosed in heaven was construed as a divine commitment to back up the authority of the church. The church took this promise as applying not only to spiritual matters but also to secular legislation. Thus all through the Middle Ages many people lived in mortal fear of the church's alleged control over their ultimate fate.

This view of the church's authority was called into question by the Reformation. A classic Protestant criticism of the misinterpretation of the power of the keys is that of Bullinger:

> Many fancy things are said about the keys of the Kingdom of God, which were handed over to the apostles by the Lord. People forge from them swords, spears, scepters, and crowns and gain omnipotence over the greatest kingdoms, as well as over body and soul. Our opinion about this is based simply on the Word of the Lord, and we say that all properly called servants of the church possess the keys of the Kingdom of heaven and exercise the power of the keys when they proclaim the gospel.[1]

Similarly Calvin held that

> this command concerning remitting and retaining sins, and that promise made to Peter concerning binding and loosing, ought to be referred to nothing but the ministry of the Word. . . . For what is the sum of the gospel, but just that all being the slaves of sin and death, are loosed and set free by the redemption which is in Christ Jesus, while those who do not receive and acknowledge Christ as a deliverer and redeemer are condemned and doomed to eternal chains.[2]

Menno Simons held the same view.

> There are two heavenly keys. . . . The key of binding is nothing but the Word . . . of God . . . by which all are included under . . . the wrath of God . . . who do not by faith receive Christ. . . .

43

> The key of loosing is the abundantly cheering and delightful Word of grace . . . and liberating Gospel of peace by which are delivered from . . . the wrath of God those who with regenerated . . . and believing hearts receive Christ and His Word. . . .[3]

Protestant reformers objected to the notion that in the promise of the keys God had written a blank check and surrendered His authority to the church. Thus Calvin claimed that in the promise of the keys "it is not so much power as ministry. Properly speaking, Christ did not give this power to men but to his word, of which he made men the ministers."[4] The power of the keys was valid only if used in accordance with the direction of God's Word and Spirit.

You Are Peter

Modern biblical scholarship has vindicated the Reformation on the interpretation of this text. As far as the role of Peter is concerned, although there are still recent commentators who suggest that the rock refers to something other than Peter himself, we can accept the statement made by Plummer already at the beginning of the century: "The first ten chapters of Acts show us in what senses Peter was the foundation on which the first stones of the Christian Israel were laid. . . . 'All attempts to explain the "rock" in any other way than as referring to Peter have

44

ignominiously failed.' "[5] This interpretation is accepted as the most natural one by Barclay,[6] and it is the one argued by Cullmann in the book *Peter*.[7] On this view the first ten chapters of Acts are the definitive commentary upon the meaning of Matthew 16:18, 19. It is simply a historical fact that through Peter's ministry God opened the door of faith to the Jews, Samaritans, and Gentiles.

This does not, of course, endorse the traditional Roman claims for the papacy. In the first place, we must keep quite clear the distinction between Peter and Christ. It is Christ who says, "On this rock I will build my church." In the words of one commentator, "The church that Jesus founds upon Peter is His, Christ's church, and not Peter's." It would therefore be a serious misunderstanding to say, as Rome has in the past, "I am of Cephas" (see 1 Corinthians 1:12), for the authority of Christ was never surrendered to Peter. Indeed, Peter exercised authority only by permitting himself to be an instrument used by Christ the builder. Nonetheless we cannot erase or obscure the fact that Jesus granted Peter a foundation place in the church for all time.[8]

In the second place, we must keep clear the distinction between Peter and his successors. In the historic sense the Apostle Peter is the one who opens the door of faith to both Jews and Gentiles. In that role he is unique and can have no successors. His place in the founding of the church can never be usurped or denied. What follows him is no longer foundation, but part of the house built *upon* the foundation. But in another sense, the apostle *must* have apostolic successors, sent ones (which is what apostolic means), missionaries and evangelists, through whom the building of the church is continued and without whom its founding and his place in its founding both come to nothing. As one scholar puts it, "The apostle has, in fact, successors, namely, the whole church. As the apostolic church it succeeds to the authority to teach, though in such a way that it must always listen to what Peter says."[9]

The Power of the Keys

In the light of this we can examine the meaning of the power of the keys and of the authority to bind and loose. The figure of keys is in keeping with the Old Testament image of the people of God as a temple or house. In Matthew 23:13 Jesus charges the Pharisees with shutting the kingdom of heaven against men, which implies their custodianship of the door of faith. According to one scholar, a scribe received a symbolic key upon ordination to his office, and in Matthew 13:52 the disciples are called scribes being trained for the kingdom of heaven. So the statement by Jesus in Matthew 16:18, 19 is a familiar one to the Jewish mind of the day. To be invested with the keys of the kingdom is to be charged with the positive task of opening the doors of salvation to all who believe, though that implies also the negative task of endorsing the exclusion from salvation of those who reject the invitation of the gospel.

The terms "bind" and "loose" have as their background the Old Testament image of salvation as a liberation from bondage. The gospels report Jesus' words at the opening of His public ministry, quoting from Isaiah, "The Spirit of the Lord is upon me, because he has anointed me to . . . proclaim release to the captives and . . . to set at liberty those who are oppressed, to proclaim the acceptable year of the Lord" (Luke 4:18, 19). The historical setting of these words is of course the deportation of captives in the exile and the hope of their liberation and return to their homeland. The words implied much more, however, than merely political liberation. In the prophetic mind they signified also deliverance from the sin for which deportation was the judgment. Behind the political bondage stood an enslavement to those sins which the prophets from Amos to Jeremiah had condemned.

If this is so, the words about binding and loosing should be interpreted as a parallel to the words about the keys. The authority to bind and loose is first and foremost the commission to proclaim the gospel, which, like the Old Testament prophetic word, liberates those who hear it,

47

though it also consigns to bondage those who reject it.

The Task of Discipling

We must conclude that Matthew 16:18, 19 does not even deal with the subject of church discipline as traditionally conceived. In the earliest church's tradition this text referred to the evangelistic mission of the church. Especially if Acts 1 — 10 is accepted as the definitive commentary on Matthew 16:18, 19, the power of the keys denotes the opening of the door of faith to both Jews and Gentiles, and the authority of binding and loosing denotes admission of people into the Messianic community. Matthew 16:18, 19 thus contains what we could appropriately call a preview of the Great Commission.

This observation is supported by the fact that John 20:19-23, a parallel to Matthew 16:18, 19, is clearly intended to be a form of the Great Commission, not only because its context is the appearance of the risen Lord, but because of the elements in the account itself. There is first the missionary mandate: "As the Father has sent me, even so I send you." And there is also the description of the giving of the Holy Spirit. Finally there are the words on remission and retention of sins, words which recall the Lukan version of the Great Commission (Luke 24:47) and Peter's words on the day of Pentecost, "Repent, and be baptized . . . in the name of Jesus Christ for the forgiveness of your sins . . ." (Acts 2:38).

If Matthew 16:18, 19 is to be interpreted as a preview of the Great Commission, how do we read the words in Matthew 18:15-18 about going to the brother? For in the latter text the encounter is clearly within the discipled community, yet in both passages Jesus speaks of the function of binding and loosing.

It is time that we relate these texts on grounds other than the mere accident of some words in common concerning the church's authority to bind and loose or to forgive sins. There is a common reality intended in these texts, which shows that the basis for incorporating people into the church is also the basis for discipline within the church. Since the church is founded upon the gospel, entrance into the community and perseverance in it rest upon the same foundation. Hence the condition laid out in Matthew 18 upon which one remains in the community is nothing other than that spelled out in Matthew 16 and John 20 upon which one enters the community.

To put it another way, the keys of the kingdom, or the authority to bind and loose, are not only a definition of the conditions for entrance into the kingdom; they also by their very nature define the ethical norms of life in the community. There is not one kind of binding and

49

loosing in evangelism or missionary proclamation, but another in discipline of the brother. In both situations the power of the keys is the good news of the coming of the kingdom and its power to open the door to life under the rule of God. *Evangelism and church discipline are both acts of discipling.*

There is, after all, only one kind of Christian existence. If there were two, then one might begin in the Spirit but continue in the flesh. Galatians 3:3. That is, there might be one answer for the problem of sin in the non-Christian, but another for the problem of sin in the Christian. Happily there is only one gospel, which alone is the totally adequate answer for sin wherever it is found. And the consequence of this is that we must undertake both evangelism and church discipline in the same way — declaring the gospel in order to bring men into the way of Jesus Christ.

Too often the meaning of the gospel, though recognized in missionary proclamation, is forgotten when it comes to discipline. Then the church is on another track — charges, courts, trials, condemnation, punishment — in short, legalism and casuistry. It forgets that what meets men initially as good news always remains for them the good news of the power of God's grace to free them from sin in order to live a life in conformity with God's gracious intention for mankind.

We can cite illustrations from church history that reveal this inconsistency between evangelism and discipline. The first is from early Protestantism. Some Protestant theologians, because of the plural of the term "keys," distinguished between the key of doctrine (signifying warning or admonition by the Word) and the key of discipline (signifying admission to or exclusion from outward privileges of the church). According to Geddes MacGregor the Scottish churchman Durham held:

> The former reaches to the thoughts and heart, and judges them, while the latter is intended "only to restrain, regulate, and judge the outward man. . . ." By the key of doctrine was meant the preaching of the Word (including private admonition, counselling and instruction, as well as sermon in Church) and the administration of Sacraments. The key of discipline comprised, strictly speaking, all the rest of the administration of the Church as a visible, institutional society, though in practice the phrase was more commonly restricted to the infliction of the various censures of the Church and their removal. . . . In the use of the key of discipline the Church condemns or approves only a man's outward practice; that is why its condemnation or approval can be absolute. It does not pretend to open or close the gates of heaven to any individual. . . . On the other hand, the key of doctrine absolutely debars from the saving promises and, on condition of faith and true, inward repentance, absolutely opens the gates of heaven. Saving grace is the condition of absolution in the exercise of the

> key of doctrine; serious profession, outward de-
> cency, is the conditon of absolution in the exer-
> cise of the key of discipline.[10]

The quotation clearly brings out an unfortunate distinction, well illustrated in the accounts
MacGregor gives of Scottish church discipline,
according to which membership in the church
and its "saving promises" was, in theory at
least, definitely "on condition of faith and true,
inward repentance," but discipline in the church
was on the basis of "serious profession and outward decency." Thus the Scottish church could
send the sheriff after people who did not voluntarily attend "sabbath" worship, or pillory in the
vestibule of the church offenders not conforming
to the church's moral standards. Such practices
were hardly consistent with the Protestant claim
that the power of the keys was a matter of the
word of the gospel alone.

A similar inconsistency is to be found in a
modern popular biblical commentator, William
Barclay. In view of the long process of reinterpretation from the Reformation to the present of
the power of the keys in Matthew 16:18, 19 and
of the authority to remit sin in John 20:22, 23
it is somewhat startling to discover in Barclay a
continuing hang-up about Matthew 18:15-18. He
contrasts this latter text rather sharply with
Matthew 16:18, 19. The importance of the issues
under discussion warrants a rather extended

quotation. Matthew 18:15-18, says Barclay,

does not ring true; it does not sound like Jesus; it sounds much more like the regulations of an ecclesiastical committee than it does like the words of Jesus Christ.

. . . We may go further. It is not possible that Jesus said it in its present form. It is far too legalistic to be a saying of Jesus; it might well be the saying of any Jewish Rabbi. Jesus could not have told His disciples to take things to the Church, for the Church did not exist, and the whole tone of the passage implies a fully developed and organized Church with a system of ecclesiastical discipline. The passage speaks of tax collectors and Gentiles as irreclaimable outsiders. Jesus was in fact accused of being the friend of tax-gatherers and sinners, and He never spoke of them as hopeless outsiders; He always spoke of them with sympathy and love, and even with praise (cf. Matthew 9:10ff; 11:19; Luke 18:10ff; and especially Matthew 21:31ff), where it is actually said that the tax-gatherers and harlots will go into the Kingdom before the orthodox religious people of the time [*sic*]. And, finally, the whole tone of the passage is that there is a limit to forgiveness, that there comes a time when a man may be abandoned by his fellow men as beyond hope, a piece of advice which it is impossible to think of Jesus as having given. And the last verse, which deals with binding and loosing, actually seems to give the Church the power to retain and to forgive sins. There are many reasons which make us think that this, *as it stands*, cannot be a correct report of the words of Jesus, and that it must be an adaptation of something which He said, made by the Church in later days, when Church discipline was rather a thing of rules and regulations than of charity and forgiveness.

It is only fair to add that Barclay continues: "Although this passage is not a correct report of what Jesus said, it is equally certain that it goes back to something Jesus did say. Can we then press behind it and come to the actual commandment of Jesus?" His commentary on the conjectured words of Jesus then turns out to be not a recovery of some original saying of Jesus, but simply a complete reversal of attitude about the text as it stands in Matthew. From it he gives a good portrait of discipline according to the gospel — "a scheme of action for the mending of broken relationships within the Christian fellowship"![11]

But why then the original strictures? In the interpretation of Matthew 16:18, 19 the presence of the term "church" offers Barclay no trouble. He explains it as "the new Israel, the people of the Lord, the new fellowship of those who believe in my name." Yet here in Matthew 18:15-18 he doesn't like the connotations of the term "church." Moreover, in Matthew 16:18, 19 the terms "bind" and "loose" give Barclay no difficulty. They refer to Peter's "administration of the church," as we see from Acts. Yet here they denote an apparently impossible "power to retain and to forgive sins."

Barclay's ambivalent attitude toward Matthew 18:15-18 shows that the issue is not the wording of the passage and also not basically whether this is a "correct report of what Jesus said," but whether these words have been rightly understood and used in much of the history of the church. For on Barclay's own second interpretation they could with no difficulty be accepted as a "correct report."

We suspect that prejudices against Matthew 18:15-18 such as Barclay's initial response represent an understandable reaction to centuries of abuse of the passage by legalistic interpretation and practice. But such a situation calls for disabuse of the passage, not a perpetuation of the misinterpretation. Barclay still labors under ancient misconceptions if Matthew 16:18, 19 means for him entrance into the community of faith by the gospel, while Matthew 18:15-18 implies continuation in the community under the tyranny of ecclesiastical legalism.

It is the purpose of this book to try to further the reinterpretation of Matthew 18:15-18 — indeed of church discipline as a whole — and to place the doctrine of church discipline once more in the context of gospel proclamation and to liberate Matthew 18:15-18 from the legalistic interpretation it has suffered since medieval times. In the following pages we will answer such strictures against Matthew 18:15-18 as those registered by Barclay in the foregoing quotation. Our procedure will be to explore each stage of the disciplinary process by constant reference to the fact that discipline, like evangelism, is an act of discipling and as such a function of the gospel. By this method we can arrive at an evangelical doctrine of church discipline.

3

IF YOUR BROTHER SINS
The Occasion for Discipline

According to Matthew 18:15 (and the parallel in Luke 17:3) the task of going to regain a brother begins with the notice of sin: "If your brother sins against you, go to him. . . ." This sounds simple enough, yet for many people it does not seem to be a sufficiently clear guideline. Does this include every little sin, such as overeating or stealing an apple? What kind of conduct merits the initiation of discipline?

These are not idle questions. The history of Christianity shows alternating tendencies toward lenience or strictness, the church at one time becoming obsessed with trivia and then again overlooking serious matters. More often the church becomes preoccupied at a given period of history with restricted aspects of life — for example, sexual morals, doctrinal beliefs, personal habits such as drinking alcoholic beverages, or clothing fashions, hair styles, etc.

Private or Public Sin

The very first question in this text concerns the meaning of the words "against you." These words have been taken by some interpreters to suggest that the procedure commanded here should be used only in the case of private offenses and that offenses of a public nature ought to be treated in a different fashion. Strangely enough the words have also been taken in just the opposite way: Zwingli held that sins warranting church action had to be offenses against the church. Private offenses were to be privately forgiven.[1]

Some scholars point out that the words "against you" may be a later addition to the text, since some of the better ancient manuscripts do not have them. Therefore they should be dropped in modern versions of this passage, as *The New English Bible* does. The parallel text in Luke 17:3 does not contain them. The words may have been inserted by an editor to whom they were suggested by Peter's question in Matthew 18:21: "Lord, how often shall my brother sin *against me*, and I forgive him?" (Italics mine.)

Even if they are genuine, the words "against you" do not necessarily restrict the range of sins calling for brotherly response. Surely a person's motive in going to the brother is not just concern for his own dignity. "Against you"

58

cannot mean merely personal affront, as though some sins have no significance beyond a private insult. All sin affects the total life of the church. If so, "against you" suggests simply that one's geographical location at a given time lays upon him, as the witness of the problem, the responsibility for accepting the initial role in dealing with what is otherwise the responsibility of the whole church as such.

It really comes down to the question of who goes to the brother, and this is more pertinent than the question of what sins he goes to the brother about. Most Christians would accept the claim that *someone* should go to the brother in need, and if the individual who knows about the brother's sin does not do so, then he should call the problem to the attention of responsible leaders in the church. Neglect is not excusable on any grounds.

The question of who should go to the brother usually focuses on the issue of whether such counseling is the function of ministers or also of laymen. In the past the tendency has been for lay people to leave this task to ministers, and too often ministers have willingly accepted it as their exclusive responsibility. Now, usually ministers have special training, skills, or gifts for counseling, but lay people should not harbor the notion that ministers possess a privileged status or authority which makes church discipline their preserve. Contemporary theology has been rethinking the role of the laity, giving much more scope once again to lay people in spiritual ministries in the church.

Whether lay people or ministers initiate the mission to regain the brother, what matters is that the whole church has a sense of being involved. In the church's evangelistic task discipling is not usually considered the prerogative of the clergy. Laymen are encouraged to witness and often do an excellent job of inviting people to accept the rule of God. Of course, when a convert makes his formal entrance into the church in baptism, the service involves the duly appointed presiding officers of the church. Nevertheless, the total enterprise of bringing people under the experience of the grace of God and into a new life belongs to the entire church.

The Problem of Secret Sin

The claim that Matthew 18 has to do with private sin suggests another common scheme that has governed the practice of discipline in some periods of the history of Christendom — that of secret and open sin. Of these, it has often been held, the church deals only with the latter.

It is fairly self-evident that no action could be taken about something strictly unknown. This does not, however, justify closing one's ears to reported sin and pretending it to be unknown, for such a matter is no longer secret. If the reporting is false or malicious, the church should deal appropriately with that problem. It should not be inferred, further, that the church needs to take note only of very specific acts of sin, and not of men's inward dispositions and attitudes, such as greed and jealousy, as if the latter do not matter. Acts of sin are related to dispositions and attitudes, and these also affect the health of the church. As one contemporary writer, Max Thurian, puts it:

> Sin, whether private or public, can never be looked upon as a mere personal shortcoming. Not only does even the most secret sin create an attitude which disturbs the peace and the joy of the community, not only has it psychological consequences which shed abroad some degree of disorder and suffering; any sin, however secret, since it is the sin of the member of the body, is a drag on the Church because it causes a rupture in her relationship with God.[2]

The problem of secret sin is not as formidable as is sometimes thought. For one thing the nature of the Christian life is such that persons cannot for long deceive themselves or others. Spiritual life is one integral reality in which sin and righteousness are mutually exclusive. Consequently even if acts of sin are concealed, the symptoms of spiritual illness will surface somewhere. Some people have the erroneous notion that sin is the positive reality and righteousness merely an absence of acts of sin. Actually, it is

61

the other way around. The discipled life is the positive reality and sin, being its absence, is the negative.

So the church does not go around looking for hidden sins. As in evangelism, so in discipline, the church goes looking for discipleship, which by its nature is open and visible. Where discipleship is missing, the church offers the remedy for the lack. The gospel is a dynamic force impinging upon the lives of people and pressing them for a response. It allows no neutrality and will inevitably receive its response, if not the obedience of faith, then its refusal. In each case the response engenders its consequences in the character and life-style of the individual being confronted by the call to discipleship. This implies that in general the best way to deal with the problem of secret sin is persistent teaching of the gospel.

We must note yet one other principle in connection with the problem of secret sin. Corresponding to the power of the gospel to manifest itself in a discipled life is its power to confer the gift of discernment. We see this gift of the Spirit to discern the thoughts and intents of the heart in the New Testament church — for example, in Acts 5 (the story of Ananias and Sapphira), Acts 8:21, and 13:10. Also in 1 Corinthians 14:23 Paul speaks of the revelation of the secrets of men's hearts. As one interpreter puts it, "Paul knows of a *charisma* which he calls 'the ability to distinguish between spirits' (1 Corinthians 12:10 f.). . . . This *charisma* constitutes therefore a presupposition of discipline.''[3]

It is not the church, but the fellow who is trying to hide sin who has got the real problem. There is no need for the church to appoint detectives to spy on sinners.[4] Where the revealing signs of sin make their appearance, the church is constrained to inquire into the life of the individual in question. But this is not a matter of prying into the private life of people; it is an attempt to help them return to the way of faith. If we make church discipline a game of hide-and-seek, it is a sure sign that we have lost sight of the meaning of discipling, which is what the whole thing is about to begin with.

Codes and Catalogs of Sin

Numerous writers in the history of Christianity have attempted to compile a catalog of sins that offers a reliable guide for initiating church discipline. Some have even sought to establish a graduated scale of sins that rather automatically triggers the appropriate response from the church — perhaps from mild admonition through public censure to full excommunication. When a given act is committed, it needs only to be classified in order for church machinery, set for the proper cycle, to be set in motion. Thus writers speak of sins as grave, flagrant, heinous, notorious, etc., suggesting a scale of degrees of moral misconduct. Corresponding to this they endorse a system of gradation in the penalties intended to deal with such degrees of sin. It is thought that small sins merit admonition, slightly more serious sins perhaps public rebuke or censure, still more serious sins suspension from communion, grave sins full excommunication, and really heinous sins the anathema. A Baptist discipline of 1774 speaks, for example, of "church censures, which differ in their nature according to the nature and degree of the offense. . . ."[5]

A little reflection persuades us that this common method of cataloging sins only leads church discipline astray. On the one hand, so-called flagrant acts of sin can be repented of and forgiven so that the sheer act of committing them does not necessarily call for an inexorable excommunication. On the other hand, what might be considered lesser sins can, with impenitence, lead to that total loss of spiritual life that ends in separation from the community of faith. In the analogous case of a non-Christian, big sins are not, after all, an insuperable obstacle, for a sinner can repent of them. Again, it takes only very little sins to keep a non-Christian from salvation if he refuses to repent.

Forgivable and Unforgivable Sin

If repentance is such a decisive consideration — the great divide in church discipline as well as in evangelism — then it would seem that ultimately we must operate with two categories. Some interpreters would find this distinction in the New Testament. First Corinthians 5:11 and 6:9, 11 have been thought by one writer to be an enumeration of "the sins which demand excommunication of the offender: immorality, greed, idolatry, reviling, drunkenness, and robbery. . . . In another letter," says this writer, "an entirely different list of sins is given, perhaps 'venial sins.' These are 'quarreling, jealousy, anger, selfishness, slander, gossip, conceit, and disorder.' These Paul rebukes though he does not immediately threaten excommunication."[6]

One might comment that if such a distinction were warranted, it would still be necessary to decide when a given act was, for example, selfishness (second list) or greed (first list). As a matter of fact, however, New Testament lists of sins are not intended to be used for this kind of classification. First Corinthians 5:11 could hardly be a list of those who are to be put out, because this might leave a thief or murderer in communion. Paul's list is simply a timely sample in a given situation.

A similar way of identifying sin calling for

excommunication is to collate and generalize from New Testament references so as to establish a kind of legal precedent. According to this method, says one writer, the New Testament justifies separation on moral or doctrinal grounds. Another claims the New Testament presents three grounds for exclusion: disruption of fellowship, flagrant immorality, and denial of the faith. Another cities three classes of sinners who must be expelled: those who live in "open sin," those who cause divisions, and those who teach false doctrine.[7] Schism, heresy, and immorality seem to be the categories that emerge from this collation and generalization, which reminds one of the second-century church's list of three mortal sins — murder, apostasy, and adultery.

The twofold classification of sins just noted reflects a valid principle of the gospel, but unfortunately it draws an invalid conclusion. It infers that a certain class of sins *per se* indicate a fall from grace and that therefore an individual's response to the gospel can be prejudged. In the case of this given class of sins the invitation to repentance can then be bypassed as unnecessary, for in effect these sins are by definition unforgivable. The corollary inference is that another class of sins is tolerable in that they do not necessitate excommunication. The tendency to classify sins generally leads to the toleration of some sinners in the church.

It is an instructive exercise to trace in the history of Christendom the development of this proclivity to classify sins as venial and mortal — that is, forgivable and unforgivable. Quite early in the history of the church the term "mortal" came to designate three specific sins or areas of sin: apostasy (idolatry), immorality (adultery, fornication), and murder. Unless apostasy was defined so broadly as to include all sin not covered by immorality or murder (and it likely was not) this threefold classification already leaves out large areas of sin — such as the greed and lying of which Ananias and Sapphira were condemned!

It appears that along with the restriction of mortal sin to these three categories came the practice of regarding them automatically as mortal, and even indelibly mortal. Tertullian held that murder, idolatry, fraud, denial of Christ, blasphemy, adultery, fornication, and every other violation of the temple of God — "admit of no pardon. . . . For these Christ will no longer plead; these, he who has been born of God will absolutely not commit, as he will not be a son of God if he has committed them."[8]

There is no reason to conclude from a reading of the New Testament that a lapse such as Peter's denial of Christ, while certainly incompatible with life in the body of Christ, inevitably called for excommunication from the church either permanently or for fixed periods of time the way some leaders of the church in the second, third, and fourth centuries thought. If the church ever adopted an ironclad rule that refused forgiveness for post-baptismal mortal sin, this practice did not long continue. The Shepherd of Hermas already argues for the possibility of one post-baptismal repentance, and in the fourth century the twice-lapsed were readmitted to communion upon their deathbed, which constituted in effect the possibility of a third repentance.[9]

In due time the Catholic Church developed its full-dress system of penance, claiming the authority to forgive even the so-called grave sins usually classed as mortal — namely, apostasy, adultery, and murder — if there was genuine repentance. The history of confessional procedure in the third and fourth centuries seems to show that the church was concerned in some sense for evidence of genuine repentance and confession. But apparently it was not concerned enough, for just as the three major sins first became automatically mortal (i.e., unforgivable) as indicated by the invariable rule of excommunication for mortal sin, so they later practically became automatically venial (i.e., forgivable) simply by virtue of three, nine, twelve, or twenty-seven years of expiation through penance, according to the dictates of the various penitential books that came into use in the course of time. This ultimate self-contradiction in the meaning of the term "mortal sin" was simply a consequence of its being moved from an evangelical to a legalistic frame of reference.

Some historians of penitential discipline commend the church of the fourth and fifth centuries for its strictness, as shown in the severity of the penances prescribed by the canonical councils. It should not be overlooked that the discipline in vogue at the time was already largely a penal code, as any reference to these penitential disciplines will show. To be sure, allowances were made. Thus, Gregory's penitential allowed that the "disposition of the party is to be of principal account."[10] That, with the continuation for a while of the practice of public confession, suggests a lingering twilight of the primitive conception of evangelical discipline.

But the fact that the disposition of the party was not of *decisive* account and that shortened sentences were *exceptions* to the rule causes us to doubt the genuineness of this apparent element of grace. On the whole the church recognized "a gradation of penalties suited to the character of the offenses. . . ."[11] Penance seems to have been increasingly a judicial sentence. When Sixtus IV in 1484 on the eve of the Reformation pronounced the church's decisions to absolve in the confessional "binding on all courts ecclesiastical and secular,"[12] and when the great ban presumed to encroach upon the civil liberties of men, this was only the fruition of a misconception that germinated at the beginning of the Middle Ages.

The misconception arose with the definition of venial and mortal as degrees of sin rather than attitudes of the sinner. Sin came to be defined within a framework of crime and punishment instead of within the framework of the gospel. Mortal sins were grave moral acts of transgression as defined by canon law. Mortal sin was no longer, as in the New Testament, sin the church was not able to forgive by reason of a lapsed Christian's impenitence. In short, because of the confusion between the church and the world with the advance of the Constantinian era, the church adopted the legalism of the state and abandoned the principles of the gospel in coping with sin among its members.

The Unforgivable Sinner

Granted the foregoing argument, is there not, some might still ask, an unforgivable sin? We would reply that if there is, it makes no difference in the initiation of disciplinary counsel, for it is precisely through such counsel that a person is discovered to be unforgivable. The essential nature of unforgivable sin lies not in the outward form of an act, as some Christians in the history of Christianity have thought, but in the mentality of the sinner. The problem is
70

not that there are some acts God cannot forgive, but that sometimes an individual places himself in a position where the power of grace does not move him. As one writer expresses it, commenting upon pertinent passages in Hebrews, "Certain states of mind secure immunity from divine grace."[13] To be precise we should not speak of an unforgivable sin but only of an unforgivable sinner.

A New Testament text dealing with this problem in the context of discipline is 1 John 5:16-18. One of the best interpretations of this passage, elucidating the meaning of "mortal sin" (RSV) or "the sin unto death" (KJV), is given by Wescott:

> In the first and simplest sense a "sin unto death" would be a sin requiring the punishment of natural death (compare Numbers 18:22). . . . If now the same line of thought is extended to the Christian Society, it will appear that a sin which in its very nature excludes from fellowship with Christians would be rightly spoken of as a "sin unto death." We are not to think of specific acts, defined absolutely, but of acts as the revelation of moral life. . . . Death is, so to speak, its natural consequence, if it continue.[14]

Clues to the meaning of this passage lie in the ban practice of the Old Testament (e.g., the stoning of Achan) and in the story of Ananias and Sapphira in Acts 5:1-11. In the cases of both Achan and Ananias and Sapphira, the sin of the offenders had literally mortal consequences.

71

They forfeited their existence in the living community. Viewed against that background, mortal sin is the loss of faith and its consequent spiritual death, and it may be connected with a variety of kinds of sin, or with no particular act of sin at all. It might more properly be termed a sin-condition.

For an instance of a sin-condition unlike that of Ananias and Sapphira, a sin *not* unto death, one could take the story of Simon Magus in Acts 8:9-24. Here, as one commentator points out, Simon was not in the state of mortal sin; hence there was scope for prayer that he might be forgiven. Peter summoned him to pray, and he besought the apostle to pray for him to the Lord.[15]

The text of 1 John 5:16-18 should be interpreted in the light of the foregoing. The prayer mentioned here is a liturgical act. Not to pray for someone who has committed the mortal sin means not to pray the prayer of absolution over him prematurely. The implication is that because of his impenitence he is not fit for restoration and thus should remain excommunicated. It does not imply irrevocable condemnation of that person or even loss of concern for him. In terms of Matthew 18 (note again the parallel with the Jewish ban) the church should regard him as a Gentile and tax collector.

To return to the original question of what kind of sin occasions church discipline — it should commence where sin as such manifests itself, and the function of initial admonition is to determine whether or not the sinner is forgivable. Where he repents, exclusion is rendered unnecessary. But where he does not repent further action is required, hopefully to awaken repentance in the offender, but also, if necessary, for the church to satisfy itself that he is unforgivable. In that event the church must excommunicate him for the sake of his eventual salvation and for the preservation of the church. As an act of discipling, church discipline brings people to decision and thereby discloses their spiritual position.

The bearing of this upon our problem is crucial. There is no possibility of compiling a complete and final catalog of sins which invite disciplinary action. Church discipline is called for by sin as such, and sin is any act or spirit inconsistent with the discipled life. Often this may not even be connected with so-called grave sins; for discipline may be occasioned by a person's coldness of heart and neglect of Christian fellowship, and it may be rendered unnecessary in the case of so-called grave sins that are followed immediately by repentance and therefore do not signify a fall from grace.[16]

This is the reason for the threefold admonition in Matthew 18:15-18. The church is most painstaking in its effort to bring to light the basic attitude of the sinner. Or, more exactly, is hopeful and eager to find repentance as an indication that the individual concerned has not fallen from grace, but that this tragedy has been averted. It looks for tokens of his continuing acceptance of the claims of discipleship. That is the index of whether he is continuing faithfully in that community which owns Jesus Christ as Lord.

The Sin of Unfaith

Strictly speaking there are not even two kinds of sin. There is only one kind, and that can be described in general terms as the absence of faith. Usually we recognize this truth in the case of a non-Christian, for there we do not assign points and add scores. Why is it so hard to see this principle in the case of discipline of the brother? Sin is purely and simply the rejection of the discipled life. Whenever it is defined in terms of casuistry the nature of sin is misunderstood and the practice of church discipline becomes unchristian.

This way of looking at sin does not mean one should hesitate going to the brother until he *has* abandoned the faith. Nor does one need to wait until there is clear and certain evidence of specific acts behind a spiritual malaise one detects. Too often in the past church discipline has been preoccupied with what are popularly called trespasses or transgressions, and has had insufficient concern for a person's general spiritual health.

Identifying loss of faith as the occasion for church discipline also does not rule out other kinds of counsel not usually classed under the term "church discipline." For example, a person with a problem of losing his temper, though not in present danger of abandoning the faith (he may have a sensitive conscience about it), can and should be given counsel on how to overcome this failing. Too often an artificial line has been drawn between acts of church discipline, formally so called, and other processes of spiritual counsel. In the end they all have as their goal the discipled life, and in many cases timely spiritual counsel can forestall the loss of faith.

The criteria for recognizing a lapse from the discipled life are nothing other than the Word and the Holy Spirit. That is, as the church undertakes its disciplinary task, it remains aware of the message of the whole New Testament, which, when used under the guidance of the Spirit, adequately portrays the nature of life in Christ and by the same token shows up the rejection of that life. The recognition of sin that invites discipline is no easier or harder than the recognition of sin that precludes baptism in someone who stands outside the church. In each case sin is simply and only an individual's refusal to follow the way of Christ. Again we are returned to our basic thesis: if response to the gospel is the condition for the admission of persons into the church — and there surely what decides is not the kind or size of a person's sin but his repentance for it — then response to the gospel must also remain the condition for the continuation of these same persons within the church.

Though the church must not become tied to a particular catalog of sins, it should, like Paul in 1 Corinthians 5 and 6, identify quite specifically conduct that is incompatible with life in Christ. On this matter modern Christians might learn a lesson from Luther, who threatened to excommunicate a man who intended to sell a house for 400 gulden that he had purchased for 30. Luther suggested 150 as a reasonable price. Inflation in this period had sent prices up, but the profit this man intended to rake off was exorbitant, and Luther, who was generally quite able to call a spade a spade, rightly labeled this piece of unbridled greed a sin that called for discipline of the church member who was involved.

In America today a church might call for disciplinary investigation of those who resist integration in the church, on the ground that one who cannot acknowledge a black Christian as his brother in the congregation of Christ has called into question his very standing in Christ and must therefore be confronted once again in church discipline with the invitation to accept the reign of God or be faced with exclusion from the kingdom.

The occasion of church discipline is sin as such. "If your brother sins, go to him. . . ." He may already be repentant, he may be wanting to repent, he may only with difficulty be persuaded to repent, or he may refuse to repent. In any case, cognizance of the peril of unfaith initiates discipline, and forgiveness or excommunication continues it. The following two chapters will attempt to trace this procedure with its two possible outcomes.

4

IF HE REPENTS, FORGIVE HIM
The Goal of Discipline

The instructions given in Matthew 18 for initiating church discipline say: "If your brother sins against you, go and tell him his fault, between you and him alone. If he listens to you, you have gained your brother." Luke says more tersely, "If your brother sins, rebuke him. . . ." (Luke 17:3). Elsewhere the New Testament speaks about the approach to an offender as "rebuke" (1 Timothy 5:20 and Titus 1:13; 2:15) or perhaps "correction" (2 Timothy 3:16).

What takes place in this approach has most often, however, been called admonition. Titus 3:10 speaks of one or two admonitions, but some traditions have it that admonition should be threefold. Perhaps this comes from the directions in Matthew 18 about three stages in a disciplinary proceeding. The prescription for this initial step in discipline seems simple enough. Unfortunately this is what has raised a problem

78

for many Christians. It is too simple, it is thought, and does not succeed in coping with the complexities of different situations. Sometimes admonition is considered too lenient, sometimes too severe. And so the church has vacillated between these alternatives throughout its history.

Hasty Excommunication

It has not infrequently been argued that there are situations where the instructions about admonition are not applicable and can be laid aside in favor of peremptory excommunication. Those who would argue thus may claim to find biblical precedent for this. They might cite Acts 5, in which Peter apparently does not pause to admonish Ananias and Sapphira, and 1 Corinthians 5, in which Paul discourages further delay in the excommunication of the immoral man. Precedent for outright excommunication can also be found in the history of the church. According to the Apostolic Constitutions, the post-apostolic church did not use the threefold admonition, at least not in the case of the cardinal sins. As noted earlier the bishop was instructed to proceed as follows:

> When you see the offender in the congregation, you are to . . . give orders that he be expelled from it. . . . Then you shall order him to be brought into the Church; and after having examined whether he be truly penitent, and fit to

be re-admitted into full Communion, you shall direct him to continue in a state of mortification for the space of two, three, five, or seven weeks, according to the nature of the offense; and then after some proper admonitions, shall dismiss [or absolve] him. [1]

The order here — excommunication, then admonition — stands in contrast with the instructions in Matthew 18 — admonition, and only if there is no repentance, excommunication.

In the time of the Reformation also there were some who held that in certain cases admonition could be dispensed with. According to the Anabaptist Peter Rideman there were two classes of sins, "those which are a cause for admonition, and those which cause excommunication without admonition, these latter being fornication, covetousness, idolatry, railing, drunkenness, theft, and robbery." [2] This is an expansion of the early church's list of mortal sins. Rideman justified this by an appeal to 1 Corinthians 5 and 6. Menno Simons had the same view when he said that whereas formerly he had "made no distinction of sins" and "spoke without differentiation of three admonitions," he had come to the view that in some cases it was "altogether improper . . . to run after [some] immoral wretches any longer with three admonitions before expulsion." His reasoning was, "With these three admonitions concerning gross offensive miscreants we would make many great hypocrites."[3] A Puritan Congregational document has the same view of the matter:

> But if the offečē be more publick at first, and of a more *heinous and criminall nature*, to wit, such as are condeñed by the light of nature; then the Church without such graduall proceeding, is to cast out the offender. . . .[4]

These references show that the urge to bypass admonition in favor of immediate excommunication is not unusual in the history of the church. It is a strong urge, and its rationale is concern to guard the witness of the church and to prevent presumptuousness on the part of the sinner. But it should be pointed out that the really serious danger to the church's witness is not the size of a person's sin, but the failure of the church to do anything about it. It would be strange indeed to consider admonition a toleration of sin when its intention is precisely the opposite — to call someone to discipleship. The truth is, the church's witness is hurt more by hasty excommunication, for then the church comes to be regarded — with good cause — as a body concerned not for restoration, but for its self-image.

Making a distinction in procedure between big and little sins is a lapse back into the early Catholic Church's distinction between mortal and venial sin, where the decisive consideration has ceased to be repentance and faith and has become instead the nature of the act as judged by some legal or moral code. The practice of invariable excommunication for what some would call major sins practically always carries with it the opposite — insufficient concern for what then are called minor sins. Such misconceptions are avoided if repentance and faith remain the basis of both individual Christian existence and corporate church life.

So admonition must not be bypassed. Every erring brother must be given a clear opportunity to repent and receive forgiveness. Only if it becomes evident that he rejects such an opportunity is excommunication warranted, and then the exclusion from the church is on the ground of his rejection of that grace which offers to remove his guilt and redeem him from the power of sin.

As for the Apostle Paul in 1 Corinthians 5 — he certainly did not violate the principle about admonition laid down in Matthew 18. Out of loving concern the offender mentioned in 1 Corinthians 5 was given an offer of the gospel with its invitation to accept deliverance from sin. Paul's reference to his previous letter (1 Corinthians 5:9-13) bears this out.

Tardy Admonition

In contrast with the practice of immediate excommunication, and in reaction, perhaps, to the judgmental attitude of the church in so much of its history, some have hesitated to speak the word of admonition at all. Was not Christ non-judgmental in His association with sinners? Did He not say, "Judge not, that you be not judged. . . . Why do you see the speck that is in your brother's eye, but do not notice the log that is in your own eye" (Matthew 7:1, 3)? Out of concern to follow what they think is the example of Jesus, to avoid self-righteousness, to avoid mistaken judgment, or to keep from offending people and thereby maybe doing more harm than good, such well-meaning Christians desist from going to a brother in spiritual trouble. They would propose that self-discipline is the right way to deal with sin in the church. Each person, they hold, must ultimately resolve his own moral problems.

A little examination will show that the teaching of Jesus in the Sermon on the Mount (Matthew 7:1-3) is no excuse for neglecting admonition. In the first place, admonition is exactly what Jesus was doing here — He was admonishing His disciples! Furthermore, His admonition was not against admonition; it was against a self-righteous way of judging. Jesus invited people to take the log out of their own eye in order to be able to help remove the speck from their brother's eye. The log was not to be retained and enjoyed as an excuse for neglecting to help the brother! This word of Jesus, then, encourages — *and exemplifies* — admonition of the brother.

All this does not, of course, minimize the importance of self-discipline, because self-discipline is essential. This is in fact the objective in going to the brother — to bring him once more to the place where he can engage in self-discipline or self-judgment. For to repent and receive God's grace is precisely the act of self-judgment. But now and then when self-discipline has broken down a person may need outside help to bring him back to the place where he is willing to engage in self-discipline, just as in physical life medical help is needed when the self-maintaining functions of bodily life fail.

There is admittedly an element of judgment present already in the act of admonition and not only in the act of excommunication. It is the preliminary and tentative assessment that a given person's conduct or spirit is not in conformity with the gospel. This initial assessment is subject to further check, as Matthew 18 teaches. It is confirmed or corrected by the response of the person in question and in addition is always subject to further review by "two or three witnesses" or on the level of the church — maybe even on the level of conference. But in any event the kind of judgment implied in admonition is in principle no different from the judgment implied in an act of evangelism or missionary proclamation, for that too tentatively judges someone to be in need of discipling, a judgment which in that case also is confirmed or corrected by subsequent events.

Admonition as an Appeal of the Gospel

Admonition of a sinner in the church is analogous to evangelism outside the church. As in evangelism repentance issues in forgiveness and fellowship, so in discipline response to the word of admonition issues in forgiveness and continued fellowship. Likewise, as in evangelism an individual's rejection of the gospel is respected and he is not incorporated into the body of Christ, so in discipline an individual's rejection of the word of admonition is respected and he is excluded from the body of Christ. The only difference is that admonition begins with a sinner in the church, whereas evangelism begins with one outside the church.

There is a danger, it should be pointed out, of a merely formal observance of threefold admonition which does not yet really operate in the spirit of the gospel. In such a situation admonition is not an invitation of the gospel but a judicial procedure, and the threefold admonition degenerates into three stages of a trial calculated to establish guilt and pass sentence. Usually a sign of such a departure from grace is the use of terms such as "filing charges," "church court," or "trial." [5]

Now to be sure the process of initiating discipline can be orderly, structured, and perhaps even formalized to some extent. But there is a danger that organization may frustrate the very purpose for which it was formed — namely, to extend the call of the gospel. Matthew 18:15 does not teach that when sin is noticed the machinery of church discipline should be set clanking in motion ruthlessly to take its course. It speaks simply about going to the brother. It might seem that a corporate institution is impartial and free from personal prejudice, but the problem is that an institution also tends to become impersonal. Church discipline requires personal involvement and concern because the gospel is always a personal appeal. "If a man is overtaken in any trespass, you who are spiritual should restore him in a spirit of gentleness," writes Paul. Galatians 6:1.

This caution about the danger of legalistic procedure does not imply that the church is not concerned for the facts or the truth in any given case. It must be very careful to avoid going on hearsay or jumping to conclusions and making false charges. At the same time church discipline is something quite other than secret service investigations and attempts at proving someone innocent or guilty. Admonition looks for the marks of discipleship. If these are present, the truth about details of any given case is no insuperable problem. If discipleship is absent, there is no point in looking for the "facts," because the fundamentally decisive fact is already given. The use of two or three witnesses, if necessary, and the hearing before the whole congregation are not primarily to establish the fact of guilt concerning the act which originally led to the admonition (though that may need to be dealt with), but to ascertain the presence or absence of faith.

Because various expressions are used in the New Testament to describe the approach to a faltering disciple, some interpreters have constructed an elaborate judicial scheme of the sort discussed in the foregoing chapter. They have therewith missed a most fundamental principle — that the initial approach in the discipling act, whether it is called admonition, exhortation, rebuke, reproof, correction, or any other term, must be seen as a presentation of the gospel. As in evangelism, so also in discipline there is only one gospel, whether people are guilty of so-called "big" or "little" sins. This gospel does not set out a schedule of penalties for a given catalog of sins, but offers deliverance from sin as such. Repeated admonition is intended to make certain that no offender in the church is denied a transparently clear invitation to discipleship and that no one is eventually excluded from the church except for rejection, in full awareness, of such an offer. It is sad to notice how absent this evangelical view of admonition has been in the history of the church.

From time to time the policy of the church has been either the severity of immediate excommunication without admonition or the lenience of tolerating sin without admonition. Both alternatives are not true to the gospel, because the gospel stands for the discipled life, and that is neither the demand for sinless perfection nor indulgence. If church discipline will be faithful to the gospel, it must begin with admonition.

The Confession of Sin

Matthew 18:15 suggests the possibility of a favorable response to the presentation of the gospel in admonition: "If he listens to you, you have gained your brother." Luke 17:3 puts it slightly differently: "If he repents, forgive him." From these words it would seem that the response desired by admonition is very simple. However, the nature of the response sought in discipline has been the occasion of much debate in the history of Christendom, debate on such questions as the sincerity of confession, whether the act of confession as such should be public or private, and whether such confession, public *or* private, requires a detailed report of the sin.

As generally used in the Bible the term "confession," like the related term "conversion," has two aspects. On the one hand is an implied or explicit admission of a wrong act or life. This is the confession of sin. On the other hand is the implied or explicit affirmation of a right way of life. This is the confession of faith or the acceptance of the way of discipleship. The Apostle Paul puts it well in Romans 10:9, 10, "If you confess with your lips that Jesus is Lord and believe in your heart that God raised him from the dead, you will be saved. For man believes with his heart and so is justified, and he confesses with his lips and so is saved."

Actually these two aspects of confession are inseparable. We can never have one without the other. If a person knows the way of righteousness, he will recognize its opposite, and if he recognizes the way of sin, that presupposes the recognition of its alternative. Of these two aspects the confession of sin may be chronologically first, but the recognition of sin becomes possible only in the light of an awareness of another option.

In the light of this analysis we can see what the nature of confession should be in the context of church discipline. If an individual has sinned, the confession which an evangelical admonition expects from him will include an acknowledgment of his failure. If he has really seen the joy of discipleship as a live option, he will no longer attempt any evasion or deception. However, this negative element in confession is never an end in itself but only an avenue to the confession of faith. Confession of sin actually has the valuable function of enabling a sinner to make a deliberate repudiation of sin in favor of the way of Christ. The ultimate evidence that a given confession of sin has fulfilled this function is a recovery of discipleship.

A church involved in discipline would therefore do well to look at the spirit and fruit of a confession rather than the quantity of details dredged up. The test of a sincere confession is not just the factual accuracy of a report of someone's past behavior, but the evidence of a new walk which shows that such behavior is being left behind. In the final analysis the church is interested in the recovery of the discipled life. And that is public and open by its very nature.

There is a serious danger in getting preoccupied with merely the confession of sin and overlooking the confession of faith. The courtroom style of dragging a confession out of somebody by cross-examination is still miles away from a truly Christian confession, because confession becomes Christian only when a person sees the folly of a given way of life in the light of the Christian way and thereby discovers the power to forsake the old way in favor of the new.

The Confession of Faith

In principle, therefore, there can be no objection to public confession. Indeed, it would seem that the natural tendency in discipline would be toward public confession, in the same way that a new Christian is expected to want to share his discovery of faith with all people. Something is wrong with a convert who is ashamed of his faith and seeks to hide it.

Reflect for a moment on this analogy of a convert. The confession he makes is primarily a confession of faith in Jesus Christ as Savior and Lord. This confession is spontaneous and joyous. It is not hidden but open — that is, freely made before all people. There is certainly present in his confession an acknowledgment of sin, because the first sign of his spiritual life is his honesty in recognizing his former sinfulness. But it is not basically a recitation of his sins, a playback of the sordid details of his life. Rather, the essential nature of his confession is a celebration of the new life he has found in the gospel.

The New Testament clearly projects this positive understanding of the meaning of confession. In the story of the lost sheep that was found, which precedes the passage on discipline in Matthew 18, and which is coupled with the parable of the prodigal son in Luke 15, there is rejoicing over the sinner that repents. The sinner, we must not forget, is *restored* to the fold. In the original setting the parables had to do with Jesus' association with tax collectors and sinners who were excommunicated from the synagogue. Today these parables are usually applied to the missionary or evangelistic situation and thus are taken to reflect someone's original salvation. But in the context of Jesus' teaching these parables applied to church discipline.

How often, alas, this spirit has been missing in the church discipline practice of Christianity. Here too often a confession is cajoled, if not coerced, rather than being elicited spontaneously. Furthermore, such a confession is frequently felt to be a humiliation rather than a celebration, and the entire affair is considered a reproach upon the congregation rather than a triumph for it. These marks betray a departure from the good news of the gospel as a basis for discipline. Where church discipline functions on the basis of the gospel, there confession is always a celebration of grace.

It appears from Matthew 18 that whether confession will be public or private may be decided largely by the stage at which an individual responds to admonition. The church of the first few centuries consistently required persons under discipline to make a public confession. There is not complete agreement as to whether this confession involved a public recitation of sins or only public acts of penance. But it is clear that the formal acts of penitence (sackcloth, fasting, almsgiving, and going through prescribed stages of restoration) were almost invariably public, as was the formal restoration or readmission of penitents in an Easter season congregational service (which suggested its parallel to the baptism of converts at that season). Later in the medieval Catholic church confession was, of course, invariably private.

In noting the practice of the church in the first centuries we must keep in mind that the confession and the restoration which followed it were always cases involving excommunicated persons. It should not be taken for granted, therefore, that cases which do not go as far as excommunication will necessarily involve public confession. If a brother heeds the private admonition, he is privately forgiven, and the matter does not call for confession before the whole congregation. Only if he refuses to heed the private admonition, and also that of the two or three witnesses, is the matter brought before the church, because the question is now one of membership itself, and this being something affecting the entire congregation, calls for their awareness. If an individual responds to the gospel in this last stage of admonition before the congregation, it will naturally be in the very nature of the case a public confession.

Matthew's prescription for dealing with an erring brother envisages this, however, as a third resort. Matthew sees the possibility, if not the likelihood, of a positive response to the private admonition at the beginning of the procedure. We may be so optimistic as to hope that most instances of discipline should be expected to terminate with the gaining of the brother at the first admonition. If so, then most instances of church discipline may also involve only private confession.

There may, of course, be other considerations in a particular case that might suggest public confession. If a person's lapse from grace is known publicly, he may wish his confession also to be known just as publicly. But there is no justification for the notion that public confession is a punishment that will serve as a deterrent. A confession will be sincere and will fulfill its purpose if it is voluntary and if it issues in the discipled life.

Forgiveness — Lenience or Severity?

Matthew 18:15 is quite terse in its description of the outcome of a disciplinary proceeding in which the word of admonition has been met by a positive response: "If he hears you, you have gained your brother." The Luke 17:3 parallel is equally brief and simple: "If he repents, forgive him." However, both texts carry the conditional "if," and Matthew 18 makes an elaboration upon the consequences of a negative response to the word of admonition. It recognizes the possibility that the individual under discipline may not receive forgiveness and may therefore enter the status of a Gentile and tax collector. Forgiveness is not dispensed automatically, but is dependent upon certain conditions.

A sense of this may be part of what lies behind Peter's question in Matthew 18:21, "Lord, how often shall my brother sin against me, and I forgive him? As many as seven times?" There follows the classic answer of Jesus, "I do not say to you seven times, but seventy times seven." And yet in the parable of the unforgiving debtor that follows, the intention of which seems to be to drive the lesson home, Jesus depicts a situation in which forgiveness is not even granted twice, let alone seventy times seven.

There are two distorted views of forgiveness possible here, and the logic of each is not hard to understand. Where forgiveness is granted only once, people are prevented from taking advantage of grace in order to indulge in repeated sinning. Where forgiveness is granted repeatedly and indefinitely, people are permitted to enjoy that unfailing mercy which can never be outlasted by sin, but is ready to greet the sinner on the other side of every failure.

Actually these alternatives are polarized against each other. Each tries to avoid the pitfall of the other. The severe alternative — setting a limit upon divine grace by refusing to excuse certain sins or refusing to go beyond a given number of forgivenesses — this intends to avoid "cheap grace." The lenient alternative — unlimited toleration of sin — this intends to avoid unrealistic demands for moral perfection.

When applied to church discipline these two views of forgiveness express themselves in quite different approaches and objectives. Whereas those who hold the strict view tend to engage in rigorous discipline, those who hold the lenient view usually hesitate to discipline at all, and whatever discipline they engage in generally offers ready absolution. In the first view, forgiveness is contingent upon moral reform because the goal is the prevention of acts of transgression. In the second view, forgiveness is granted unconditionally because the goal is to magnify divine mercy in the face of inveterate human failure.

These two respective views of forgiveness can be observed in the history of church discipline. In most of post-apostolic and early Latin church history there were only one or two forgivenesses granted. A Christian who violated them through post-baptismal sin was not allowed further forgiveness; he was bound and not loosed "till he should pay all his debt." But by the end of the Middle Ages, with the rise of mandatory annual confession, the church which claimed succession to Peter was listening to Christ's other word to Peter; it was prepared to offer forgiveness seventy times seven, and that led merely to indulgence.

Each of the views we have sketched usually appeals to one strain of thought in the New Testament. The view that sets a limit upon forgiveness will cite passages such as 1 John 3:4-10. This text, it is held, demands perfection. However, the epistle of John, it is not hard to show, does not demand moral perfection. This is made clear by the words, "If we say we have no sin, we deceive ourselves" (1 John 1:8). The epistle does say, "No one born of God commits sin; for God's nature abides in him, and he cannot sin because he is born of God" (3:9). But that this does not mean sinless perfection is plain from the expression, "God's nature abides in him." John is not contrasting mere sinlessness and sinfulness. He is contrasting the person indwelt by God's nature with the one not thus indwelt.

The view that forgiveness implies toleration of sin has been a much more formidable one, in both Catholic and Protestant traditions. In Protestantism this view usually seeks support in the doctrine of justification by grace through faith in the Pauline writings. Too frequently this Pauline formula is interpreted as an indulgence for sin. After all, the man of faith, though justified, is still a sinner. In Lutheran terminology, he is simultaneously justified and sinner. Paul, of course, never meant, nor Luther either, that justification implied a toleration of sin. The explosive, "God forbid!" of Romans makes this clear. What Paul meant was that the justified sinner is one who has received a totally new quality of life by virtue of his openness to grace. What the apostle is talking about is a new nature. Justification is therefore not a divine game of "let's pretend," in which God is kidding Himself that an obvious sinner is really righteous. Justification means a living relationship through which God's grace transforms the believer's life.

In support of the notion that justification is a "legal fiction" some writers appeal to Paul's letters to the Corinthians. Paul twice calls the Corinthian Christians sanctified (1 Corinthians 1:2; 6:11) though they are notorious for their immoral conduct. Hence it may be concluded that saintliness is for Paul after all only a theoretical truth, or at best his hope of better conduct by his converts in the future. Such would be a gross misunderstanding of the situation. Paul twice calls the Corinthian Christians sanctified because they are *in fact* new creatures in Christ. That is the basis upon which he communicates with them. Where the new nature is not a reality — as shown in the absence of a response in one individual to the apostle's appeal — there Paul calls for excommunication. 1 Corinthians 5. The unholy person is to be put out because he evinces no signs of spiritual life. His lack of sorrow or repentance is only further evidence of the absence of spiritual sensitivity — a fact first indicated by the immorality itself. It must be conceded that Paul does expect a cessation of sin; so the goal of moral improvement cannot be denied. However, moral growth, more properly called sanctification, invariably finds its place within the qualitative distinction between faith and unbelief.

Justification by faith as understood popularly in Protestantism has made it very common to say that the church is a home for sinners. In a sense this is true. But we must remember that *repentance* for sin is the condition of membership in the church, not sin as such. Admittedly the church is a home for sinners, and like a home is intended as a place where training or rehabilitation takes place, precisely through discipline. Or in Augustine's figure, the church is a hospital, but only those who acknowledge need of a physician go there, and then to get well. People who die are removed from a hospital. The hospital must not be turned into a morgue! Under a different metaphor it is sometimes said that the church is a "school for sinners." Then, presumably, willingness to learn, to become a disciple, to be disciplined, is the condition of enrollment.

Forgiveness — A New Nature

Our discussion of the meaning of forgiveness shows another possibility beyond the false alternatives mentioned — demand for moral perfection or cheap grace. It is genuine forgiveness. The big obstacle has been to see forgiveness as a commercial transaction rather than as a relationship. Perhaps the cause of this is a Protestant preoccupation with the law, as a result of which forgiveness then tends to be only forensic. Forgiveness is never, however, merely a position before the law. It is a new relationship with God and consequently also with people. In Jesus' terms it is an entrance upon the way of the disciple who lives in expectation of the coming rule of God. In Pauline terms, forgiveness is an appropriation of the Christ-nature.

In this light forgiveness is no concession to human weakness, but a celebration of divine love and power and the realization of a new quality of life. As one theologian writes:

> The forgiveness of sins is the basis, the sum, the criterion, of all that may be called Christian life or faith. . . .
> Christian life is the life which takes a man out of himself and introduces into him the principle of divine life. Understand Christian morals as you wish . . . provided your life is situated on this movement of transfer from God to you and from you to God; provided the exchange between God's life and your life takes place. . . .
> A passage from Paul sums up what we have just said. Galatians 2:20: "It is no longer I who live, but Christ who lives in me; and the life I now live in the flesh I live by faith in the Son of God, who loved me and gave himself for me." If

we understand this verse, we have understood everything. This is the whole of faith and of Christian life. [6]

We can conclude our discussion of the meaning of forgiveness in church discipline by returning to Matthew 18. When Jesus enjoins Peter to forgive seventy times seven, He implies that forgiveness is not a demand for sinlessness. When He tells the parable of the unforgiving debtor, He shows that forgiveness is not indulgence of continued sinfulness. Forgiveness is the realization of the discipled life. In discipline, as in evangelism, the church seeks nothing more and settles for nothing less. Where admonition is received by the hearing of faith, there forgiveness is achieved. Where it is met by persistent impenitence, there the church is obliged to speak eventually the word of excommunication. It is to the discussion of this latter we now turn.

5

GENTILE
AND TAX COLLECTOR
Redemptive
Excommunication

According to Matthew 18 if a brother under discipline refuses to heed the word of admonition, the church is to take further action.

> But if he does not listen, take one or two others along with you, that every word may be confirmed by the evidence of two or three witnesses. If he refuses to listen to them, tell it to the church; and if he refuses to listen even to the church, let him be to you as a Gentile and a tax collector.

Most interpreters take this to mean excommunication. In the eyes of Judaism the Gentile was someone outside the community of faith, and the tax collector signified one who by compromise with the Gentile world had apostatized from the community of Israel and was therefore banned. Hence the obvious meaning of the text seems to be exclusion from the church.

Is It Christian?

Some writers on the subject of church discipline question, however, whether the practice of excommunication is supported in the New Testament or found in the primitive church. The prevailing tone of the New Testament message, they say, is forgiving love, and this would be contradicted by an act of judgment such as excommunication. Thus one scholar says:

> A painstaking exegesis makes clear that the church did not know of a formal excommunication. The case of the deliverance to Satan (1 Cor. 5) has to do with a direct intervention of the Lord. In all other cases it is the church or congregation that withdraws, separates itself, and suspends table fellowship. And that is not the same thing as excommunication. These nuances are not incidental.[1]

This concern is shared by several European writers on discipline who feel the term "excommunication" has picked up meaning from the practices of the church in the history of Christendom — things like coercion and civil punishments — that are inconsistent with the teaching of the New Testament.

Excommunication is not, of course, a biblical word, but then neither is its root, communion. Unless we are prepared to abandon that term as well, the issue is whether excommunication will be defined according to the message and spirit of the New Testament or according to unevangelical practices in the history of Christendom. It seems undeniable that Matthew 18 and other New Testament texts envisage an act that can be called excommunication. The nature of this act has been described by one writer thus:

> When unfaithful members of the church plainly declare by their actions that they choose rather to obey the laws of Satan than the commands of Christ; . . . when men have by their own choice and by the actions of their life in effect placed themselves outside her communion, the church solemnly and formally ratifies their own deed and refuses to receive them back until they repent and testify their desire to be restored again to a state of salvation. [2]

If excommunication should not be called a *formal* act, it seems logical to infer that the act of baptism and reception of someone into the body of Christ should also not be recognized as a formal act, because excommunication is really the reverse of baptism. Yet we generally do not object to considering baptism a formal act. We must therefore also recognize the formal act of excommunication, because they are correlatives.

The church is also tempted to run away from the responsibility of excommunication, if and when this becomes necessary, because it is a painful task. The danger in rationalizing that there is really no such thing as a formal excommunication is that it pretends the problem of sin in the church will go away by itself.

There has, unfortunately, been bad excommunication practice, and this has conditioned the thinking of many people to the point where they can see nothing redemptive in the dismissal of a member from the church. Therefore it is essential to see that excommunication does not represent a breakdown of grace or a departure from the gospel. Excommunication is a renewed presentation of the gospel message to an impenitent brother in that it confronts him with the truth Paul states in 1 Corinthians 6:9, "The unrighteous will not inherit the kingdom of God." To utter this truth in warning to those who have apostatized is just as consistent with the nature of the gospel as informing people in evangelism that unless they repent and believe the gospel they will not enter the kingdom of God. Thus excommunication, rightly practiced, never cuts people off from grace. On the contrary, its function is to prevent persons from anesthetizing themselves against grace. Excommunication is the form under which the church continues to make grace available to the impenitent.

Excommunication is not, then, merely loveless condemnation. It is as necessary in spiritual life as candid diagnosis is in medical practice. Without facing the truth persons cannot find spiritual healing. Far from being unloving, evangelical excommunication is the only loving and redeeming course of action possible in given circumstances.

Fencing the Lord's Table?

Historically one of the persistent problems in church discipline has been the relationship between excommunication and communion. Sometimes suspension from communion has been considered a first step on the way to full excommunication, and sometimes it has been considered already the full equivalent of excommunication, perhaps because communion is for many churches the central symbol of membership and participation in the body of Christ.

Strangely enough, there are two opposite tendencies on this matter. On the one hand, some people advocate leaving the Lord's Supper open to those who have sinned and are under discipline, even making a special effort to have them participate. The rationale for this is that the Lord's Supper is the means of grace, and who needs this more than the impenitent sinner? Continued access to the means of grace, it is alleged, may bring him to repentance. On the other hand, some advocate withholding communion from those under discipline because their participation would desecrate the Lord's table, harm the witness of the church, and bring damnation upon the sinner because of unworthy participation. 1 Corinthians 11:27-32.

An answer to this apparent dilemma must begin with a proper understanding of the meaning of the Lord's Supper. The Lord's Supper is a confessional act in which people who present themselves at the Lord's table declare to each other and to the world that they stand in covenant relationship with God and that they accept the consequences of this covenant — namely, forgiveness and fellowship. Thus it is appropriate that all who have covenanted discipleship should participate in the enacted confession of this covenant. And conversely, all who participate should manifest the life of discipleship it bespeaks. If this is so, then participation in the Lord's Supper on the part of an impenitent sinner is an obvious contradiction, since his act of participation in communion is inconsistent with his life. Such a person is a living lie. He may try to deceive himself about it — and others too — but sooner or later his hypocrisy will exact its judgment. It is a fundamental law of life that people who indulge in self-deception eventually destroy themselves.

In the light of this, and to prevent a brother from "eating and drinking judgment upon himself," many believe the proper course is to withhold communion. A little reflection will show, however, that this has an undesirable implication, for if participation in communion is a repeated act of confession of faith, then suspending someone from communion is to pronounce him faithless! That is, banning someone from the Lord's table is equivalent to excommunicating him from the community of faith. But the danger in suspending someone from communion is that it peremptorily cuts an individual off, as in precipitate excommunication, without offering him the admonition of the gospel. We have already noted the imperative of such admonition.

However, usually suspension from communion is not intended to signify full excommunication. It signifies instead that a given person is not in fact the faithful disciple that his participation in communion would profess, and yet it makes room for continued communionless membership in the church, implying that there is possible a second level of membership on a basis other than the appropriation of new life in Christ. In this latter implication it merely repeats in slightly different form the misunderstanding of the other policy of condoning impenitent participation in communion. Where lenience makes room for faithful and faithless communing membership, strict suspension makes room for faithful communing and faithless non-communing membership. Both arrangements suggest two kinds of membership, two levels of existence in the church — forgiven and unforgiven.

This surely is not an acceptable system. In what direction can we look for a better one? I would suggest the examples of Jesus at the Last Supper and of Paul in 1 Corinthians 5. Writers on church discipline like to point to Judas among Jesus' disciples, and they observe that Jesus even invited him to the Last Supper despite His knowledge that Judas had defected and would betray Him. From this they conclude that the church must tolerate sinners in its midst. It is sometimes debated whether Judas did or did not receive the elements at the supper. However, whether or not bread and wine entered his digestive system is irrelevant. The crucial thing was the challenge to faithful discipleship that met Judas in the bread and cup and the decision he made in response to it. The sop was an invitation to change his mind and remain a member of Jesus' community — a most awesome admonition. Judas could have made the decision to heed this admonition by the act of eating in good faith. But he rejected the invitation, as is shown by his departure, and by this decision he was exposed and effectively removed from the community.

There is no truth, then, to the claim that Jesus tolerated a hypocrite among His disciples. But neither did He begin by excluding him from the supper. Jesus began with an encouragement to Judas to participate, though with the clear understanding that participation with integrity called for a radical about-face in thought and deed. The situation was so structured as to combine loving concern with the demand for an honest decision. The Lord's Supper was thus the setting for an attempt at re-discipling, or disciplining, a hypocrite — which ended, alas, with a negative decision. As applied to the life of the church, this example of Jesus may show how discipline can actually take place in the context of communion, for communion becomes the invitation to discipleship and the setting in which persons by the nature of their response are brought to decision.

Paul in 1 Corinthians 5 followed a procedure that at first sight seems the opposite of what Jesus did at the Last Supper. Whereas Jesus offered Judas continued communion, Paul called for cessation of communion — "not even to eat with such a one" (1 Corinthians 5:11). Between the two situations there is an underlying difference, however. The case in 1 Corinthians 5 is beyond the stage of discipline at the Last Supper. Here was a man who presented himself repeatedly at the Lord's table while refusing to quit an immoral life. Since he was unable or unwilling to resolve this self-contradiction himself, the church had to declare to him that it could not be partner to his hypocrisy by continued communion with him. He was informed of his condition by being excommunicated.

It is not hard to see the fundamental difference between the biblical principles we have here attempted to sketch and the practice of the church in much of its history. In discipline according to grace the church does not arbitrarily begin with suspension from communion, but with an increasingly fervent appeal of grace. If this appeal goes unheeded, the church out of love does not, however, permit the individual to destroy himself unwarned. Indeed, the church resorts to excommunication to safeguard the meaning of that gospel by which alone people must be saved.[3]

In some cases of church discipline the issue of communion may not arise, especially if it is celebrated infrequently. Then discipline problems may be settled between communion seasons. But if the problem arises, the church must beware of precipitate acts of judgment on the one hand and condoning indefinite hypocritical participation on the other hand. In either case the church hurts itself, the individual, and the cause of the gospel in the world. Church membership normally implies attendance at communion, and we must remember that a person under admonition is still a member of the church. Only if he refuses to heed the admonition of the church is he excommunicated — that is, simply and completely excluded from membership in the body of Christ. As a "Gentile and tax collector" he is then once more the object of Christ's call to discipleship.

Major and Minor Excommunication

When suspension from communion is distinguished from total excommunication, it suggests degrees of excommunication. For a good deal of its history the church has spoken specifically of major and minor excommunication, or the greater and lesser ban. Sometimes the anathema was added as a third and most severe degree of excommunication, though usually it was regarded as an aggravated major excommunication. A Catholic writer states "that in former times the ancient Christians knew nothing of the system of major excommunication."[4] In the light of this it is interesting that since 1884 the Catholic Church holds to only major excommunication.[5]

Martin Luther was opposed to the major excommunication of the Catholic Church of his day on the ground that it belonged to the secular order. He believed the church had a right to use only minor excommunication.

> We consider the greater excommunication, as the pope calls it, to be merely a civil penalty which does not concern us ministers of the church. However, the lesser (that is, the truly Christian) excommunication excludes those who are manifest and impertinent sinners from the sacrament and other fellowship of the church until they mend their ways and avoid sin. Preachers should not mingle civil punishments with this spiritual penalty or excommunication.[6]

What is to be said to this question? In the discussion above on church discipline and the Lord's Supper we maintained that there are not two levels of membership in the church, faithful membership with communion and faithless membership without. It is even more absurd to propose that there are two levels or degrees of non-membership! Although room must be made for a time for people struggling toward a decision, ultimately the gospel postulates only two positions, faith or unbelief. The question of degrees of excommunication is settled if we remember that basically the dismissal of a person from membership in the church is a declaration of the gospel. It shows a person the gap between his life and true discipleship. Every action a church takes beyond this declaration of the word of the gospel is punitive.

The medieval notion of major and minor excommunication arose through a confusion of the church and the state. Inasmuch as people were members of the church, excommunication entailed the suspension of religious privileges. But inasmuch as Christianity was officially established, excommunication logically constituted also the suspension of people's civil rights — such things as citizenship, guild membership, and so forth. Hopefully anyone who understands the gospel does not propose to go back to that!

Even today there are always numerous ways, some of them perhaps quite subtle, in which members of the church could, however, inflict punishment upon excommunicants. Although we have a separation of church and state in America, and people of our churches may not even know medieval terms such as major excommunication, nevertheless it is possible to ostracize someone socially, boycott his business, or in some way discriminate against him. This resort to punitive measures can never achieve commitment to the Christian way.

Destruction of the Flesh

There frequently arises, in connection with the subject of excommunication, the question of the meaning of an expression appearing twice in the New Testament, in 1 Corinthians 5:5 and 1 Timothy 1:20, "delivered to Satan." In 1 Corinthians is added the phrase, "for the destruction of the flesh." It might be suggested that these expressions do imply a punitive element beyond a simple declaration of the gospel to an unrepentant person. This invites the further question of whether the instructions in 1 Timothy 1:20 and Paul's counsel according to 1 Corinthians 5:5 are at variance with the dominical pattern laid down in Matthew 18, with its more passive, "Let him be to you as a Gentile and a tax collector."

Most scholars interpret Paul's expression somehow or other to mean simply excommunication. A representative biblical commentator states:

> Delivering to Satan apparently signifies excommunication (see verses 2, 7, 13). The idea underlying this is that outside the church is the sphere of Satan (Eph. 2:12; Col. 1:13; 1 John 5:19). To be expelled from the Church of Christ is to be delivered over into that region where Satan holds sway.[7]

And a writer on church discipline commenting on 1 Timothy 1:20 says that handing people over to Satan means "to put them for a time outside the communion of the church, that is to say into the realm of the princes of this world of darkness so that, deprived of the special grace of the community, . . . they may realize the consequence of the error of their ways."[8]

It might nevertheless be argued that "delivering to Satan" suggests more than treating someone like a publican and a sinner, especially if the former phrase is taken with its 1 Corinthians 5:5 concluding phrase, "for the destruction of the flesh." The action described by Paul seems to some interpreters to imply the positive infliction of a sentence and not merely the passive surrender of an impenitent person. Some writers interpret "destruction of the flesh" to mean consignment to physical suffering, perhaps even death. It has been suggested that Paul was resorting to a technique used by people in the pagan religions of the time.

> A person who had been wronged by another and had no other way of retaliating, consigned the criminal to the god, and left the punishment to be inflicted by divine power. In the invocations, the god was asked or expected to punish the wrongdoer by bodily disease; thus any bodily affliction which came on the accused person was regarded, by both the invoker and the sufferer, as the messenger or weapon of the god.[9]

It can be said categorically that there is no reason for reading such ideas of vindictiveness into Paul. The act of handing an individual over to Satan was precisely a refusal to retaliate, a determination to leave judgment to God.

Some writers, noting the words, "That his spirit may be saved in the day of the Lord Jesus," suggest that Paul is working with a doctrine of purgatory. They cite 1 Corinthians 3:13 and 11:32 as further evidence of Paul's belief that sin may be expiated by temporal suffering and that elect souls who endure it will thereby be saved at the last day.

Now the suggestion of a connection between sin and sickness is not unthinkable. There does seem to be a hint of such a connection not only in the story of the healing of the paralytic (Matthew 9:2-5) but also, and especially, in James 5:13-18. The subject is worthy of a study in itself, but here we can only point out that while forgiveness may lead to healing and, conversely, unforgiven sin may lead to sickness and suffering, such sickness, suffering — and even death — do not necessarily lead to forgiveness.

It is beside the point to look for complicated explanations of Paul's thought and action, because the conception he has of a "destruction of the flesh" has for its background the experience of baptism and regeneration. In Romans 6:6, for example, Paul says, "We know that our old self was crucified with . . . [Christ] so that the sinful body might be destroyed," and in Colossians 3:5 he says, "Put to death therefore what is earthly in you. . . ." Surely we are not to see here the infliction of physical suffering! Then it is also not necessary to read it into 1 Corinthians 5:5.[10] "Destruction of the flesh" and "salvation of the spirit" are correlative. "Destruction of the flesh" means "the annihilation of the demonic powers and the sinful self that has handed itself over to them," and flesh signifies "everything in us which is in thrall to the power of sin because of our passionate and perverse propensities."[11] "Destruction of the flesh" was supposed to have been realized already at the baptism of the individual referred to in 1 Corinthians 5:5. But his repudiation of grace obliged the church to make the new offer of grace through the shock treatment of excommunication, in the hope that this might achieve that destruction of the sinful self and the salvation of the spirit which had somehow not yet been realized.

All this does not suggest that the sin and rejection of grace for which the church excommunicates someone may not lead to suffering. Nor does it suggest that such suffering might not be used by God. As we have noted above, not to submit to the reign of God in Christ is to put oneself under the rule of Satan and sin. And the wages of sin is death. However, in the body of Christ the Spirit delivers people from the body of death and gives them life. Romans 7:24; 8:2. I would maintain, therefore, that "destruction of the flesh" in 1 Corinthians 5:5 does not supply a basis for an excommunication practice intending physical suffering. As one author says, deliverance to Satan "is neither the imposition of a civil penalty nor the infliction of bodily pain," but "simply expulsion from the Christian society."[12] This is how it was understood also by the early Puritans in a congregational confession of 1589.[13]

We can safely conclude that deliverance to Satan does not imply a severe form of excommunication, and it is absurd to suggest that Paul is not following the example of the gentle and loving Jesus. *The Interpreter's Bible* asks: "Was Paul insisting upon a wise course of action? Would Jesus have done this, or would he have been more merciful toward the sinful?" This invites the rejoinder that Jesus did, in fact, do precisely what Paul here advises, and is likely Paul's example. Jesus' dealing with Judas is nothing other than a deliverance to Satan, even if it did not apparently achieve his ultimate salvation.

We would hold, then, that 1 Corinthians 5:5 is not a case of a serious form of excommunication. Rather, it shows how serious excommunication is. It is better to take this passage into account before formulating an understanding of excommunication as a whole than to bring to it a preconceived notion of excommunication in order to find here an aberration. Paul teaches us that excommunication is serious business.

Anathema Maranatha

Although the connection of an "anathema" with excommunication is not as clear in the New Testament as "delivered to Satan," an anathema was associated with excommunication in the Middle Ages. According to one authority, "during the first centuries the anathema did not seem to differ from the sentence of excommunication (but) beginning with the sixth century a distinction was made between the two . . ." Excommunication signified separation "from the society of the brethren," and anathema separation "from the body of Christ, which is the church." The anathema came to be defined as an especially solemn excommunication. Pope Zachary (731-752), in drawing up the formula for the ceremony of anathema, distinguished three sorts of excommunication: minor, major, and anathema, "or the penalty incurred by crimes of the gravest order, and solemnly promulgated by the Pope." [14] An anathematized person could still, however, repent and be absolved.

Luther is reported to have spoken of praying the Lord's Prayer against an excommunicated person, and this prayer was to wreak unhappiness upon its object, but he seems to have equated this with the deliverance to Satan of 1 Corinthians 5:5, the text we have just discussed.[15] Calvin followed the Medieval church in distinguishing excommunication from anathema, but he differed with it in claiming that "the latter, completely excluding pardon, dooms and devotes the individual to eternal destruction." The anathema, he added, "is rarely if ever to be used."[16]

Although its connection with discipline is quite tenuous in the few New Testament texts mentioning it (Romans 9:3; 1 Corinthians 12:3; 16:22; Galatians 1:8, 9), the anathema has a meaning in biblical thought that is not inconsistent with the gospel. That meaning is rooted in the Old Testament practice of devoting objects or people — especially the enemies of Israel — to the judgment of God. But the curse could also fall upon a member of Israel who coveted some accursed thing and therefore had to be removed from the living community of Israel. When the death penalty ceased being imposed, in the evolution of discipline practice in Judaism, execution was replaced by a symbolic funeral ceremony, which betokened the spiritual death of an Israelite in being cut off from the people of God.

In the New Testament Paul uses this language from his Jewish heritage when he says, in 1 Corinthians 16:22, "If any one has no love

for the Lord, let him be accursed." We can con-
cur with the commentator who remarks upon
this text: "The world was divided into two classes, those who loved, with however many fail-
ings and backslidings, the Lord Jesus, and those
who hated Him. It is the latter who are anathematized." [17] That is, they are committed to
the realm lying under the curse. Between the
garden of Eden, where the curse descends, and
the New Jerusalem, where it is lifted, the world
lies under the curse. Now Christ bore away the
curse, and His deliverance becomes effective for
those believing in Him. Those, however, who
do not love Him still lie under the curse. Paul's
simple twofold classification in 1 Corinthians
16:22 would seem to indicate that an anathema,
strange as it sounds to modern ears, and despite the colorings it has received from church
history, is simply synonymous with excommunication. There is no justification for introducing
once more punitive and legalistic connotations
from outside the gospel.

With this background we have a basis for
examining the significance of the Ananias and
Sapphira story of Acts 5, which is often raised
in connection with discipline because it is
thought, rightly, to be a case of anathema.
There is a clear parallel between this story and
that of Achan in Joshua 7. In each case the sin
of greed invades the pristine community, in
each case there is a supernatural disclosure of

guilt, and in each case the culprit is removed from the community by a divinely sanctioned sudden death.

Jean Lasserre finds it surprising that Calvin sees in Acts 5 justification for the occasional use of physical punishment by the church. When it comes to the gospel miracles Calvin thinks we have a phenomenon restricted to the primitive era of the church, says Lasserre. "But astonishingly enough [Calvin] never asks himself whether the miraculous punishments too may be strictly confined to this period. . . . It cannot be admitted," adds Lasserre, "that they are part of an ecclesiastical discipline for which they would be normative models." But since Calvin insisted on finding guidance for discipline in Acts 5, Lasserre asks, "Did he himself ever administer physical punishment to an adversary by the power of his words alone?" Acts 5 will not cover up "the capital executions of which the church, alas, has carried out all too many, with or without the hypocritical aid of the secular arm."[18]

As an instance of church discipline, Acts 5 does not require us to resort once more to punitive notions inconsistent with the gospel. God has the right to intervene and take life at any time, early or late, through either so-called natural or supernatural means, even if that cuts off for some individuals the day of opportunity for repentance. But the point is exactly that this is an exercise of the divine prerogative, and hence it is not necessary to postulate instances in which the church pronounces an excommunication of such gravity that it bears the kiss of death. Nor is it necessary to postulate certain forms of excommunication that preclude the possibility of repentance. Even the Jewish curse left room for repentance, as did the Medieval church's anathema. The Ananias and Sapphira story symbolizes the spiritual death entailed in excommunication. Theirs is a case of mortal sin, and it stands in the tradition as a warning to the Christian community, as the story of Achan does to Israel.

6

WARN HIM
AS A BROTHER
Avoidance and Restoration

The subject of excommunication sooner or later raises the question of avoidance, popularly called "shunning." The suggestion is logical because avoidance has to do with the treatment of an excommunicated person. To many people avoidance or shunning is an eccentricity of narrow-minded religious sects, but more careful investigation will show that some form of avoidance has a firm base in the New Testament. It seems to be implied by the reference in Matthew 18:17 to treating someone like a Gentile or tax collector, though this must be squared with the claim that Jesus did not avoid tax collectors and sinners but ate with them.

In addition to Matthew 18:17 there are several other New Testament texts that can be cited as authority for avoidance.

> Take note of those who create dissensions and difficulties, in opposition to the doctrine which

you have been taught; avoid them (Romans 16:
17).

I wrote to you not to associate with any one who
bears the name of brother if he is guilty of immorality or greed, or is an idolater, reviler, drunk-
ard, or robber — not even to eat with such a one
(1 Corinthians 5:11).

Keep away from any brother who is living in
idleness and not in accord with the tradition that
you received from us. . . . If any one refuses to
obey what we say in this letter, note that man,
and have nothing to do with him, that he may be
ashamed. Do not look on him as an enemy, but
warn him as a brother (2 Thessalonians 3:6, 14).

For [in the last days] men will be lovers of
self, . . . lovers of pleasure rather than lovers of
God, holding the form of religion but denying the
power of it. Avoid such people (2 Timothy 3:2-5).

As for a man who is factious, after admonishing
him once or twice, have nothing more to do with
him (Titus 3:10).

This is a forceful array of texts. They show that
avoidance cannot simply be written off as a custom of sectarians. It must be reexamined and
defined in the framework of a truly Christian
discipleship.

Social Ostracism?

One interpretation would have it that avoidance, at least one form of it, is a mild kind of

discipline short of full excommunication. 2 Thessalonians 3:14 especially seems to lend itself to this interpretation. Thus one writer says on this text:

> There is no necessary suggestion of excommunication. Probably some kind of separation is implied. It is not that the man is to be separated from the church, but rather that the church is to avoid the man. It seems at least reasonable to infer that . . . the offender might while still enjoying such church privileges as he cared to avail himself of, be treated with a certain coldness, ostracized socially if not yet ecclesiastically. Or an act of discipline may be implied, the man being refused communion for a space. But no definite conclusion can be reached from such vague premises.[1]

A Puritan Congregational conference of 1589 took this view. It interpreted 2 Thessalonians 3:15 to mean "sharply reprehend" and "gravely admonish" an offender "prooving if at any time the Lord will give him repentaunce." Puritans were to practice avoidance also, however, of a fully excommunicated person; warning was given to the congregation "to abstaine themselves from his societie."[2]

The inclination to interpret 2 Thessalonians 3:14 as a mild form of avoidance short of full excommunication likely comes from the clause in the verse which says, "Warn him as a brother." Does "brother" describe the attitude desired in the admonisher or does it indicate the status of the person being admonished? No conclusive answer can be reached from an examination of the grammar of this passage alone. There is another clue, however. It can be shown that the word for avoidance used in this text (*sunanamignusthai*), which occurs only three times in the New Testament, is the same as that employed twice in 1 Corinthians 5:9, 11, where its meaning is rather well established as a relationship involving excommunication.

In line with our definition of the discipling task up to this point we contend that rejection of the gospel is the decisive ground for breaking fellowship. It is in fact the only thing that *can* disrupt fellowship. For that reason it would seem that the conception of avoidance as an ostracism within the church is inconsistent with the nature of the church. As long as an individual is a brother, fellowship with him is normative. Only if he ceases to be a brother is this fellowship broken, and then the very breaking of it becomes a reminder to him that he has ceased to be a brother, and as such it becomes also an invitation to return. Recourse to an ostracism in the absence of complete excommunication moves once more in the direction of major and minor excommunications, a view we discussed earlier and found incompatible with the gospel.

Is there, however, a place for avoidance in the case of full excommunication? Some groups in Christendom, chiefly the early Dutch Mennonites, the early Church of the Brethren, and the Amish, have made avoidance a rather severe ostracism following excommunication. Such avoidance, they have held, reaches even into the natural relationships of home and family. Menno Simons held that "the rule for the ban is a general rule, and excepts no one; neither husband nor wife, nor parent nor child."[3] Alexander Mack, founder of the Church of the Brethren, also supported the practice of avoidance. He cited Deuteronomy 13:6-9, according to which members of an idolater's own family should be the first to raise their hands against him to stone him, and Matthew 10:37, which warns, "He who loves father or mother more than me is not worthy of me." Like Menno Simons, Mack allowed, however, that one could contact excommunicated persons in order to admonish them to repent and also to help them in case of physical want.[4] Is this the kind of shunning intended by the biblical texts quoted at the beginning of this chapter?

Avoidance Is Communication

The central significance of avoidance can be gathered from Jesus' words about treating someone like a Gentile and tax collector. We must not forget that the tax collectors and sinners spoken of in the Gospels were excommunicated from the Jewish community; so Jesus' attitude toward them is the model of Christian avoidance! If the clue to the meaning of these words is the conduct of Jesus Himself, and I think it is, then avoidance treats the excommunicated person as a prime candidate for the call to discipleship, but this also implies unambiguously, let us not forget, that his present standing is outside the kingdom.

In other words, avoidance is that kind of circumspect relationship with an excommunicated individual which brings home to him the truth about his spiritual condition and does not permit him to escape into self-deception. It means refusing to pretend that a person is a Christian after he has ceased to be one. It means respecting his decision and honestly treating him once more like a person of the world. But like excommunication it constitutes a form of continuing to present the gospel.

Avoidance must clearly say two things simultaneously, first, that a given individual has forsaken the way of discipleship and, second, that he has a standing invitation to return to it.

Avoidance, then, is a process of communication and not, as some might infer from the word "excommunication," cutting off communication. It is also not a system of punishment, of coercion, of blacklisting, or of ostracizing someone as a social outcast. Rather, it is the appropriate way of presenting the invitation to discipleship to someone who presently stands in the position of having renounced it. But discretion is needed in this task. If, on the one hand, the church must not cut off communication, it must also, on the other hand, not mix its signals so as to cancel out the message of the formal act of excommunication. A backslapping camaraderie can easily contradict what the church is saying by its formal excommunication, and this inconsistency only confuses an excommunicated person, leading him to deceive himself about his condition and anesthetizing him against the call of the gospel.

Avoidance is concerned for clear communication not only with such a person but also, of course, with other Christians in the church and with non-Christians in the world. If some Christians by their conduct failed to acknowledge the practical implications of an excommunication, that would tend to mislead their fellow Christians and unbelievers as well. It would suggest to them that a lapse from the faith and its consequent excommunication do not really change a person's actual condition. Thus it would encourage people on all sides to kid themselves and each other that nothing serious is amiss. The consequences of something like this are understandably disastrous for the total cause of the Christian community.

Paul's teaching in 1 Corinthians 5:9 supports the meaning of avoidance we are sketching here. When the apostle enjoins the Corinthian church not to eat with a persistent sinner, he is talking primarily about the Lord's Supper. He is counseling discontinuation of those associations which could be construed as continued or resumed Christian fellowship by the excommunicated individual, other Christians, or the world, and the sacramental supper is naturally the crucial issue. He immediately warns against drawing ridiculous conclusions from his counsel on avoidance (see 1 Corinthians 5:10), and elsewhere he goes on record as holding no objection to secular table fellowship (1 Corinthians 10:27). Nevertheless in the Corinthian correspondence as a whole he repeatedly warns Christians against the sort of relationships that would mislead fellow Christians, deceive themselves, or obscure the church's witness to the world.

One added thought. From what has been said it is evident that an effective and truly Christian practice of avoidance presupposes public excommunication. The purpose of this is not, of course, to pillory someone. Officials in the church may try to keep an excommunication private for the best of intentions, chiefly to protect an individual from public disgrace, but obviously only confusion can come when church members are kept in the dark about someone's lapse from the brotherhood. Excommunication must be public because it involves an altered relation between an individual and every other member of the church. Congregational involvement is important because of the reality of inter-personal relationships entailed by church membership.

This argument is in line with the tendency in recent theology to encourage congregational participation in the rite of baptism, for this also involves a new pattern of relationships between the new member and every other person in Christ's congregation. Excommunication is, in a sense, a reversal of baptism. As at baptism the whole church under its Lord acknowledges the act of faith, endorses Christ's incorporation of this individual into His body, and becomes Christ's agency in the incorporation, so here the whole church acknowledges the act of unfaith, endorses Christ's exclusion, and becomes the agency of that exclusion.

Marital Avoidance?

An understanding of the basic meaning of avoidance enables us now to evaluate the kind of strict shunning that includes familial and marital avoidance. Jesus claimed that spiritual relationships sometimes cut directly across the natural relationships of life. "For I have come to set a man against his father, and a daughter against her mother . . . and a man's foes will be those of his own household" (Matthew 10:35, 36). This is usually taken to apply to what may happen through conversions, but it may also happen through excommunication. Thus an individual may need to recognize that an unfortunate apostasy places his own parent, spouse, or child outside the church. But this recognition of a pattern of spiritual relationships cutting across natural ones reminds us that these are not to be confused. In rigid shunning, as in familial and marital avoidance, they are confused, since a break in spiritual fellowship between an individual and his relatives is thought to demand a break in natural relations. A careful reading of 1 Corinthians 5:9-13 makes clear that Paul's whole counsel rests upon a recognition of the distinction between spiritual and natural associations. Indeed, its purpose is to bring this home to someone who has lost sight of this distinction and mistakenly considers himself still in Christian fellowship by virtue of certain continued social relationships.

On the issue of marital avoidance, and in connection with 1 Corinthians 5:9-13, we should read also 1 Corinthians 7:12-16, because the latter passage deals with the same problem, though it is there treated in the context of conversion. Some well-intentioned new believers in Corinth thought the spiritual gulf between them and an unbelieving spouse called for the abrogation of the natural relationship of marriage. Not so, replied the Apostle Paul. When a married person becomes a Christian but his spouse does not, he should not seek to get divorced. In fact, the continuing natural association is seen as the occasion for a life of witness to the unbelieving spouse. Similarly in excommunication a gap in spiritual relationships does not call for the abrogation of natural associations, a de facto divorce. Rather, natural associations are the means for pointing an individual back to the opportunity of spiritual life. True avoidance is not disuse but discreet use of natural associations and relationships for this spiritual end.

Avoidance, then, is only a continued reminder of what excommunication itself already declares. It is a sensitive and tactful use of social relationships to confront an individual with the meaning of the gospel. It may be true that the biblical passages on avoidance we have discussed do not specifically name excommunication, but the absence of mention of bell, book, and candle does not mean the principle is not involved.

Restoration

As we have stressed repeatedly, when Matthew 18 speaks about someone's reversion to the position of a Gentile and tax collector, this makes him once more a candidate for discipleship. Now and then in the history of the church it has been suggested that excommunication is an irrevocable condemnation. In the face of such suggestions it must be stated most emphatically that excommunication, being a presentation of the gospel, by its very nature implies the opportunity for restoration. There may be no reference in Matthew 18:15-20 to such a restoration, though the preceding verses (18:10-14) speak of the return of the lost sheep. We know that in the Jewish community the doors were open to restoration of even a person who had fallen under the great ban and had been considered as dead. And Paul's counsel in 2 Corinthians 2:5-11 is an instruction to restore an individual with whom church discipline has achieved its purpose. (Whether or not this is the person mentioned in 1 Corinthians 5 is beside the point.) A restoration is envisaged also in 1 Timothy 1:20. Unless "may learn not to blaspheme" in this passage is merely vindictive, it can only mean coming to the obedience of faith under the admonition of discipline.

In the post-apostolic age of the church there were those who allowed no room for repentance and restoration of excommunicated persons. But it was not long before the Catholic Church readmitted penitents who had been guilty of even so-called mortal sins, though for some centuries only one such restoration was permitted. What is of interest to us here is the restoration procedure of the church during the era of public penance, especially since, in contrast to the New Testament, which says very little concerning penitential procedure, it prescribed a relatively elaborate ritual of penance. As mentioned earlier, there were three or four stations of penance through which excommunicated penitents passed. For the first year they were

> excluded entirely from the whole service, and were to stand weeping at the church door, which was the Station of mourners; in the year following, they were admitted to that of hearers; in the third to that of the Prostrate, called [properly] the penance; the fourth they were permitted to stand with the faithful whilst they communicated, but might not themselves partake with them. . . . At last, they were restored in full to all their privileges, and were allowed to communicate.[5]

The duration of the sentence varied in different penitential books.

What seems to us most noteworthy is the suggestion in these books that genuine repentance is practically incidental, even though some also say that "the disposition and temper of the party under discipline are of principal account."[6] Thus one canonical epistle prescribes for murder nine years at each of three stations; if there is true repentance, the second and third stages may be reduced to eight, seven, or five years.[7] In Basil's penitential the penance for a woman who aborts is ten years, though he says, "Let their treatment depend not on mere lapse of time, but on the character of their repentance."[8]

The question persistently arising in the face of this is: Why was the individual, if truly penitent, required to serve time at all? Or, Why should an individual repent at all if time alone would reinstate him, seeing "true repentance" merely *reduced* the time? In later centuries the order was reversed: whereas at first the church imposed penance, then absolved, it later absolved and then imposed penance. If the sinner was paying for his sins, why not on credit? The fact that in later centuries penance did not usually involve excommunication does not alter the fact that the reversed order showed how true repentance had lost its importance.

Both the early practice of disallowing any restoration and the later system of restoration through acts of penance reveal that the condition of membership in the church was no longer the discipled life. First permanent exclusion, regardless of spiritual attitude, and then later restoration through penance, regardless of spiritual attitude, show the church had moved away from life in Christ as the basis of discipline.

There was an insight that the early church had which might have saved it this departure from the gospel into legalism, had the church followed the implications of that insight. Where it did permit a restoration, the church of this era regarded such restoration of a penitent as a sort of second baptism, seeing it signified an event in its nature parallel to baptism. Thus penitents were classed and seated with catechumens and were absolved at the Easter baptismal season. This parallel between restoration and baptism shows us the true conditions of restoration. They are simply the authentic marks of spiritual life. In one sense this certainly is a condition or requirement. The church is "satisfied," if we can use the term, only with the discipled life. But this rules out meritorious acts of satisfaction (in the usual sense) as definitely in restoration as it does in original admission to the church. One writer perceptively notes that penitential requirements were never laid upon new converts, either in the New Testament or in the history of the church. [9] So if we have a double standard between baptism and restoration, we can be sure that one or the other of them is misunderstood and maybe both.

The perennial temptation of the church is to demand more for restoration than for baptism, to make the conditions for restoration higher than for original incorporation into the body of Christ. It is afraid the Lord might be too lenient and needs protection against those who might take advantage of His grace by sinning again. According to Matthew 18:21, 22 this problem occurred to Peter when he asked, "How often shall my brother sin against me, and I forgive him?" In Christ's answer Peter is instructed not to set any limits upon divine grace. God Himself is the guardian of grace and is quite able to protect Himself against the hypocrisy of men. Where He grants men repentance and the gift of faith, there the church must be prepared to be the ministering agency of forgiveness. To add other conditions for restoration beyond genuine discipleship only hurts the cause, because it moves the church from its foundation in the gospel.

At times in its history the church has been just plain punitive in its restoration procedure. Occasionally the early church went so far in its penitential discipline as to forbid a restored adulterer to "resume the cohabitation of marriage."[10] Sometimes too it permanently barred persons from return to office in the church. Now it may be necessary to exercise discretion in appointing restored persons to office (and it should be appointment by virtue of spiritual fitness, not automatic reappointment) just as discretion is justified in the case of new converts. But it is inconsistent with forgiveness to hold restored members in a state of perennial disgrace, or to make them "pay" with continued humiliation, or to put them on any other probation than that under which all believers always live.

It should be remembered that the restoration we have in mind is the readmission to fellowship of an individual over whom the church has been constrained to speak the evangelical excommunication defined in the preceding chapter. Such an excommunication is a decisive event, and for that reason the restoration of a penitent individual is to be distinguished carefully from the absolution of one who responds to admonition before excommunication. Earlier we noted that excommunication calls for the participation of the church. By the same token an individual's restoration to spiritual fellowship calls for congregational recognition, not just to invest the forgiveness with public sanction, but to permit cognizance on the part of all members of the church of the real change of relationship taking place between a restored individual and themselves.

Nonetheless, there is not one kind of forgiveness sought by admontion and another by the more drastic means of excommunication and restoration. There is only one gospel, and only one kind of spiritual life it offers. Hence in the readmission of excommunicated persons, as in all other aspects of the life of the church, if forgiveness is forgiveness at all, it is that one and only kind of forgiveness the gospel knows — the kind that issues in the discipled life.

7

THE WHEAT
AND THE TARES
The Visibility of the Church

Some reader might very possibly suggest that the foregoing ideal in church discipline can never become a reality in practice because of the invisibility of the church. We have all heard some form of the claim that only God knows saints from sinners. We finite men cannot tell who are among the elect. The problem would seem to be accentuated especially if, as we have maintained in the previous pages, the basis of discipline is not a legal code but spiritual life. One can identify acts of transgression, but isn't it presumptuous to claim to read men's hearts? The true church is invisible, goes the argument, and does not coincide with the visible organized institution on earth.

It is not hard to see that this line of thought effectively paralyzes discipline. At most one could admonish a brother who *seems* to be failing according to the best of our judgment, though even this might be completely gratuitous if we can't really tell. Certainly no binding action can be valid, since one might excommunicate a person whom God has not excommunicated or, on the other hand, forgive a person whom God has not forgiven.

It should be recognized that this line of thought also undermines the practice of baptism and the existence of the church itself. If we cannot tell who is a true Christian for purposes of discipline, we can't tell in evangelism either. The logical consequence of the claim that the church is invisible is that we don't know whom to baptize. We can have no meaningful membership lists. The whole enterprise of building the church is then a game of blind man's buff.

But we do baptize people into the membership of the church, and we do this, we are convinced, on the basis of authentic faith. If this is not so, our churches are merely social clubs with no necessary relation to God's saving action — in which case nothing about the visible church ultimately matters. But if life in Christ is the condition of membership in the church, as practically all churches in Christendom hold, then the act of taking people into membership signifies that we consider such life in Christ discernible.

In short, if faith is really not discernible, whom are we trying to kid by having churches? The existence of churches indicates that we believe there is some correlation between God's grace and the visible church, in which case those must justify their claim who say that there is no such correlation. The conviction with which almost all Christians operate — that membership in a visible church is significant — is itself evidence that they hold true faith and discipleship to be visible. If this is so, what is needed is a clarification of this underlying conviction and its application to the problem of discipline.

An adequate discussion of the subject here under examination must deal with the biblical passage which more than any other tends to be used to call church discipline into question. Time and again in the debate over discipline writers will find in the parables of the wheat and the tares (Matthew 13:24-30, 36-43) and of the dragnet (Matthew 13:47-50) scriptural and dominical authority for questioning the practice of discipline, or even for invalidating altogether some aspects of discipline such as excommunication.

Tolerating Hypocrites?

The predominating interpretation of the parable of the tares — we could almost call it the classic interpretation — can be indicated by a quotation from John Calvin:

In my opinion, the design of the parable is simply this: so long as the pilgrimage of the Church in

143

the world continues, bad men and hypocrites will mingle in it with the good and upright, that the children of God may be armed with patience, and in the midst of offences fitted to disturb them may preserve steadfast faith.[1]

The most important thing to be noted in Calvin's interpretation is the application of the parable to the church, which is of special significance in view of the fact that Calvin, unlike most modern scholars, doubtless took the Matthean interpretation (which explicitly applies it to the world) as the words of Christ Himself. When the parable is thus applied to the church, it tends to contradict the church's mandate to exercise discipline. A contemporary scholar presenting this line of thought is Joachim Jeremias. In a book on the parables he says:

> The idea of a premature separation is expressly rejected, and patience until the harvest is enjoined. Why is such patience necessary? Jesus gives two reasons. First, men are not capable of carrying out the separation effectively (Matt. 13:29). As, in the early stages of growth, darnel and wheat resemble each other, so do true disciples and false believers. Men cannot discern the heart; if they attempt to make an effective separation, they will inevitably commit errors of judgment and root up good wheat with the tares. Secondly, and more important, God has fixed the moment of separation. The measure of time assigned by him must be fulfilled (Matt. 13:47) . . . the seed must be allowed to ripen. Then comes the harvest and with it the separa-

> tion between tares and wheat. . . . But that moment has not yet arrived. . . . Till then, all false zeal must be checked, the field must be left to ripen in patience, . . . and everything left to God in faith, until his hour comes.[2]

According to this line of thought one *cannot* judge and one *must not* judge. One *cannot* because it is not possible in this world for human eyes to distinguish the righteous from the unrighteous. One *must not* judge because it is not yet the time and also because it is not man's prerogative to do so. It will be accomplished in God's time and way by the instrumentality of the "angels." This seems to be supported by Christ's statement: "Judge not, that you be not judged" (Matthew 7:1), especially if taken with Paul's "do not pronounce judgment before the time" (1 Corinthians 4:5).[3]

The traditional interpretation sketched above has the effect of throwing the teaching of the parable of the wheat and tares into contradiction not only with the clear injunction to practice discipline which Jesus gives in Matthew 18 but also with the clear practice of discipline in the apostolic church (e.g., 1 Corinthians 5).[4] Did Paul in 1 Corinthians 5 become impatient and judge before the time? More seriously, did Jesus contradict Himself on this point? One writer accurately poses the problem: "Here the servants are forbidden to weed and bind, while later [in Matthew 16 and 18] the disciples are allowed to bind."[5]

145

Numerous writers seem disturbed at this apparent contradiction and feel obliged to resolve it. Explanations have been tried in several directions. One method of approach is frankly to admit a contradiction and to allow one of the opposing points of view to be more or less canceled out. This seems to be the approach of one writer, who points to Jesus' own apparently nonjudgmental attitude (in John 8:1-11 and with Judas), and argues furthermore that the few New Testament passages seeming to support firm church discipline cannot stand in the way of the prevailing spirit of unfailing mercy in the New Testament. According to this writer the parable at least rules out all excommunication. [6]

An alternative approach has been the attempt to explain that the parable applies only to certain kinds of sins. Thus, love must excuse fleshly weakness, but not false teaching and coarse sins, thought Zwingli. [7] Or the church is obliged to tolerate only hypocrites, or those whose conversion is not hopeless, not manifest and obstinate offenders, says another writer. [8] Or again, one should root out only for heresy and scandal. [9] There is, however, no basis in this text for such a discrimination.

A little reflection shows that the traditional problem of reconciling the parable with church discipline arises from a faulty interpretation. To begin with, the parable never implies that saints cannot be distinguished from sinners. In fact, the very meaning of the entire parable rests upon the assumption that they clearly can be. In the parable the servants were not suspecting a malicious act and looking for tares. They pointed out to the householder something expressly forced upon their attention. From this one thing can be accepted as settled: the problem is not inability to discern the tares, because discerning them only too well is what gives rise to the problem. The central question in the parable, which even a cursory reading shows, is what to do with this existing recognizable problem. That is, in view of a patently weedy field, how is a desired — and even necessary and inevitable — separation to be achieved?

Archibald Hunter suggests that the parable of wheat and tares "sounds like Jesus' reply to a critic — probably a Pharisee (the very name meant 'separatist') who had objected: 'If the Kingdom of God is really here, why has there not been a separating of sinners from saints in Israel?''[10] Jeremias writes in a similar vein: "Everywhere in the time of Jesus we meet with attempts to set up the Messianic community. . . . The Pharisees clearly claimed to represent the holy community.''[11] And some Jewish authorities were quite in favor of weeding sinners out, as we can see from the story recorded in John 8:1-11, according to which they wanted to stone the woman taken in adultery. There were others also like Simon the Zealot or James and John (in Luke 9:54) who "with an irreligious solicitude for God . . . wanted to accelerate the Kingdom's advance by direct action."[12] They sought to achieve the reign of God by the use of violence and terrorism as the Pharisees sought to impose it with law and order.

Gathering the Harvest

To all such approaches Jesus gave His decisive answer. The kingdom of God cannot be established by coercion or violent destruction of the unrighteous. But does Jesus' rejection of the violent and coercive methods advocated by others mean that the mixed community must be forever endured, that a righteous community cannot be realized until the end of the world? Much interpretation goes astray at this point because the harvest Jesus talks about ("the close of the age") is identified by interpreters with a still future final judgment at the end of time.

It must be observed, however, that Jesus considers His coming to be the close of the old age and the advent of the new. The harvest is therefore most imminent. As C. H. Dodd says, "It does not seem necessary to suppose that the judgment is treated as a new event in the future," because "as we have seen, the coming of the Kingdom of God is in the teaching of Jesus not a momentary event but a complex of interrelated events including His own ministry, His death, and what follows, all conceived as forming a unity."[13] Although the opening verses of Matthew 13 liken the proclamation of the kingdom to the process of sowing, other passages, as Dodd shows, illustrate the coming of the kingdom under the figure of harvest.

> Significantly enough, this interpretation finds support in the Fourth Gospel. The Johannine equivalent for the Synoptic saying, "The harvest truly is plenteous," is to be found in the words, "Lift up your eyes and behold the fields, that they are white unto harvest" (John 4:35). The whole context reads as follows: "Do not say, 'Four months yet, and the harvest comes.' Behold I say to you, lift up your eyes and observe the fields, that they are white for harvest. Already the reaper is taking his pay, and gathering a crop for eternal life, so that the sower and reaper may rejoice together. For in this the saying is true: 'One sows and another reaps.' I sent you to reap that on which you have not laboured. Others have laboured, and you have entered into their labour."[14]

From the foregoing observations it becomes clear that the parable of the wheat and the tares means almost the opposite of what it is usually taken to mean. Instead of a rejection by Jesus of the attempt to establish a pure community, it is His statement of the only way to establish such a community. There is a sensible way of separating wheat from weeds, a way of establishing a separated, righteous community which embodies the rule of God. But it is not the way of violence. It is the way of harvest, the old God-ordained and time-honored way of gathering people through missionary proclamation. If the seed that has been sown is left to do its work, it will come to fruition in God's time and way. Jesus warns His followers that the only legitimate and possible way of establishing the kingdom is to proclaim the word, gather the righteous, and leave the wicked to the divine wrath.

This is the only possible interpretation of this parable, for if there is no separation till the future judgment, then there can also be till then no Great Commission, no gathering of the harvest, no missionary reaping, no church. But there was a Great Commission given, and there exists a church in the world. It stands as a witness to the separating work of the gospel of the kingdom.

The parable of the seine net is usually considered parallel to that of the wheat and the tares. Jeremias says "both parables . . . are concerned with the Final Judgment which ushers in the Kingdom of God; it is compared to a separation." However, "God has fixed the moment of separation. The measure of time assigned by him must be fulfilled . . . but that moment has not yet arrived."[15] This interpretation leaves incomprehensible the statement in the parable that it is the fishermen themselves who sort out the fish.

A much more natural and coherent interpretation of this parable is given by C. H. Dodd:

> Now the point of the story is that when you are fishing with a dragnet you cannot expect to select your fish: your catch will be a mixed one. . . . But — there is after all a process of selection; . . . there is a sifting of possible followers of Jesus. . . .
>
> Here then we have an interpretation of the parable which brings it into line with the other sayings of Jesus, and relates it to the actual course of his ministry. The Kingdom of God, in process of realization in and through that ministry, is like the work of fishing with a drag-net, for the appeal is made to all indiscriminately, and yet in the nature of things it is selective; and, let us recall, this selection *is* the divine judgment, though men pass it upon themselves by sheer ultimate attitude to the appeal.[16]

We can now draw our conclusions on the meaning of these parables and their bearing upon discipline. They have a bearing upon discipline only indirectly, since they are concerned primarily with the calling out of a righteous community through missionary proclamation. But since, as we have maintained all along, church discipline is based upon the gospel, these parables do not discourage the practice of discipline. They teach how church discipline should be carried on — by the use of the word of the gospel, and not by the use of coercion and violence.

Rudolf Bohren is one of the few scholars who discerns the correct meaning of the parable of the wheat and tares and hence its bearing upon the subject of church discipline:

> The parable and the explanation discuss the relation of the disciples to the surrounding world, not, however, the relation of the disciples with each other. . . . Church discipline shall not become world discipline.
>
> Jesus then did not fight against Church discipline. One may not play off the parable of the weeds against Church discipline.[17]

That expresses it: "Church discipline shall not become world discipline." It must not be imposed by the church upon the world, and it must not be worldly in its nature. Expressed in positive terms, church discipline should be exercised only by the church, and only upon the church.

There is more than a little irony in the fact that some of those in the history of the church who were most eloquent in their appeal to the parable of the tares in the traditional way were the very ones who failed to hear its real message. Augustine appealed to the parable in his controversy with the Donatists, arguing for Catholic tolerance against the Donatist demand for stricter separation of the righteous. But then he endorsed the suppression of the Donatist heresy by imperial force.[18] And Calvin, as we noted above, pleaded for tolerance in the name of the parable, but then did not allow himself to be dissuaded from helping to uproot one particularly obnoxious tare — Michael Servetus — that seemed to stand in the way of the establishment of God's kingdom in Geneva.

One of Calvin's contemporaries, Menno Simons, was aware of the real meaning of the parable, perhaps because, with a price of 100 gulden on his head, he happened to be one of the "tares" the Roman Catholic Church of the Netherlands was trying to uproot, and so learned the meaning of the parable from hard experience.[19] Martin Luther also interpreted the parable rightly:

> In this parable the field is the world. The wheat means the good children and the tares the bad. . . . We are not to be affrighted by this because the devil is always among the children of God. As for the treatment of these heretics we are here told that we are not to exterminate them, since he who errs today may turn to the right course tomorrow. Who knows if the Word of God will touch his heart? But if he is burned or strangled, he is prevented from coming to the truth and thus he is lost who might have been saved. The Lord points out furthermore the danger that the wheat will be destroyed along with the tares. See, then, how frightful we have been that for so long we have handled the Turks with the sword, heretics with fire, and have sought by killing to force the Jews to the faith, to root out the tares by our own power, as if we were the people to rule over hearts and spirits. I would rather tolerate an entire unChristian land

for the sake of one Christian in the midst than to exterminate one Christian with the unChristians.[20]

Doubtless the main reason for the abuse of the parable in the long history of Christendom is that the field was identified with the church, even though the interpretation given in Matthew says that the field is the world. This is partly understandable in view of the fact that the church was for most of the Constantinian era identified with the European world. Nevertheless, church and world constitute the distinction against which alone the parable makes sense and under which alone the church can obey the teaching of the parable and allow the gospel of the kingdom to perform its function of establishing and maintaining the community of faith.

Postulating an invisible church and then conveniently confusing the church and the world usually leads to one or more deplorable consequences. Sometimes the church tries to preempt the power of the secular world and insists that its discipline supersedes civil or even criminal law. This is the pattern that developed in the Middle Ages. The jurisdiction of the church "came to be recognized as good not only in the forum of conscience, but in the secular courts."[21] Sometimes the church expects the secular authorities to relieve it of the responsibility of discipline. This was unfortunately too common in the state churches of Protestantism, as we have noticed earlier. Sometimes the church tries to divide legal responsibilities between itself and the secular order, classifying sins and dealing with "religious" ones itself (e.g., adultery) and leaving "civil" matters to the state (e.g., business ethics). The answer to all these confusions is the recognition of a visible church and therewith its distinction from the world. Then the church is able to go about its discipling task in corrective discipline as in evangelism — according to norms derived from the gospel. The other option — that is, postulating an invisible church — almost invariably leads the church to confuse its discipline with secular law.

A Visible Church

The parable of the wheat and the tares would not have been such a problem in the history of the church if the doctrine of an invisible church had not been read into it. For that reason it might be useful to add a few remarks about the problems inherent in this doctrine. Emil Brunner claims that this doctrine came into western theology through Augustine, whose study of the New Testament taught him that the biblical idea of the church was something quite different from what he saw around him in the all-inclusive institutional Catholic church. But both were called the church; so to distinguish them Augustine used the terms "visible church" and "invisible church." According to Brunner the Reformers Zwingli and Calvin "took over this fundamental concept," but he goes on to say that this concept of the church "is wholly foreign to the New Testament."[22]

That the term "invisible church" is an anomaly and does not really mean one cannot tell who is a true Christian becomes clear through only a moment's reflection. For the distinction between the visible church and the invisible church rests on the observation that obviously, patently, visibly, not all in the institutional church are true believers. If the invisible church really were invisible, one would have no basis for distinguishing it from the visible church.

The real problem in church discipline is not that of being able to discern the true saints but of what to do about the contradiction between the New Testament norms and the existing situation. This is supported by the comments of several contemporary theologians. For example, Gerhard Ebeling admits that the practice of discipline is inextricably bound up with the definition of the boundaries of the church. If it is impossible to speak of the boundary of the church, he says, then it is not permissible to speak of church discipline.[23]

Ebeling rightly notes that God defines the boundary of the church, and he rightly notes further that this act is recognized by faith. But then, realizing that many members of the established institutional churches of western Christendom do not possess living faith, he decides that faith is not after all definitive for membership — that baptism alone (and he means infant baptism) is the basis of membership in the church. Consequently there are two kinds of belonging, he asserts, confirmed and unconfirmed, confessing and non-confessing — in short, faithful and faithless. He speaks of membership of the positive mode (those who attend worship and sacrament) and of the negative mode (who have never formally left, and still pay taxes). He justifies this distinction by an appeal to the New Testament distinction between the weak and the strong, the primitive church distinction between catechumen and baptized, the old Catholic distinction between Christian and penitents, and Luther's between the masses and earnest Christians.[24]

We might remark that the visibility of the church and the discipline it entails are not dependent upon so-called believer's or adult baptism. For pedobaptist churches also seek to define their existence ultimately by faith. To achieve or even retain full membership, persons baptized as children must be confirmed. That is, they must themselves evince living faith.

As a matter of fact, the major Reformers opposed a system of levels of membership, at least in principle, on the ground that faith was the one constitutive ground of the church. And yet levels of membership are often freely admitted and sometimes even justified and encouraged. Bonhoeffer, usually noted for his emphasis on discipleship, writes:

> Whereas baptism characterizes the congregation's wish to spread God's Lordship as widely as possible (that is, it characterizes for us the fact of the national church), the congregation gathered for preaching is composed of those personally placed before the decision of accepting or rejecting the divine gift; it is both a national and a gathered church. At the Lord's Supper the church presents itself purely as a gathered church, as a confessing congregation, and is required and acknowledged as such by God. It does not, however, represent the pure *sanctorum communio*; it is the smallest of the three concentric, sociologically distinct circles, and is both the source of the church's effectiveness and equally on the other hand the focal point of all its life.[25]

This is a bold defense of faithless membership in the church and as such advertises the fact that the issue is not the discernment of the faithful but what to do about the faithless.

Our contention that the church is visible does not mean one can predict who will become saints in the future — that is, ultimately be numbered among the elect. The boundaries of the church are continuously changing, and no man can expect to divine where they will ultimately stand any more than he can control where they will stand. Nevertheless, God's congregation, there where God has called it out and set it in the midst of the world with the task of gospel proclamation, can affirm and endorse where response to the gospel is setting the boundaries from time to time; and it asserts that these boundaries are of saving significance.

Furthermore, the claim here made for the visibility of the church does not mean a Christian can recognize any and all saints any strange place on earth, nor that he can recognize them at once. It does not even suggest that error may not creep in despite considerable observation. But it does mean that the discipled Christian is always recognizable, and therefore questionable cases are subject to investigation and correction. No amount of sophistry touches this point, which can be shown by an illustration: because a man may not be able, under certain circumstances (e.g., 29 1/2 minutes after sunset, at 333 feet, with 15-20 vision, in a slight rain), to recognize his own brother does not mean he cannot confidently identify him under average circumstances. The question is whether and how he will investigate if the person in question really is his brother. Here the illustration becomes a parable. Faith is solicitous to know and be assured of the faith of others. And faith also seeks to make itself known to others. This conviction lay at the heart of the "watch and care" of early Methodism. Wesley said:

> I had been often told it was impossible for me to distinguish the precious from the vile, without

> the miraculous discernment of spirits. But I now
> saw, more clearly than ever, that this might be
> done, and without much difficulty, supposing only
> two things; first courage and steadiness in the
> examiner; secondly, common sense and common
> honesty in the leader of each class. . . . The
> question is not concerning the heart, but the
> life, and the general tenor of this I do not say
> cannot be known, but cannot be hid without a
> miracle.[26]

The rejoinder might still be made, and well so, that there is always a margin of church members over whom there is some question. Granted that there are those on the one hand who show no fruit of the spirit in their lives nor even show any marks of repentance, and on the other hand those whose life leaves no doubt about their discipleship. But neither of these groups is a problem. The problem arises with those in the church who are in the gray area in between.

What is sometimes not noted carefully enough is the fact that the exercise of discipline itself presupposes a margin at the boundary of the church over which there is a question. Regardless of how wide or narrow this margin is considered to be, there are always some individuals coming or going about whom there is question. Discipline, beginning with admonition of those who seem to be failing to manifest spiritual life, admits uncertainty over these people.

But the question is: What shall be done about the margin of professing church members in question? Some say we can and should do nothing. They argue that the church is invisible, therefore we can never judge, except for guesses, and then our judgment carries no further than the external form of the earthly institution. The consequence of this is a paralysis of discipline.

We would argue that the margin over which there is question — the hazy boundary between obvious saints and obvious sinners — is actually an argument for discipline instead of against it. If faith ought to be openly confessed, and if there are some whose faith is in question, this situation calls for inquiry. That is, people over whose status the church is in doubt are invited to make their commitment to discipleship unambiguously clear, and if they do not, they must, in love, be warned that they are deceiving themselves about their salvation. Else those in the church who should know better are guilty of failing to define the meaning of discipleship and are abetting people's self-deception.

Discipline begins with concern for people whose spiritual condition stands in uncertainty. It does not expect to finish its task so as to achieve once and for all an absolutely "pure church." A static church with a fixed and unchanging boundary would not be a living church. The healthy church is one that is faithful in discipling people and, one hopes, expanding the boundaries of the church. Where the church is not faithful in working at the narrowing of the margin over which there is uncertainty, there a backlog builds up and the margin grows. When this margin comes to comprise the majority, there the church is in a real plight. It then must return to the task of evangelism. But this, as we have seen, is once more the act of discipling people.

8

BINDING
AND LOOSING
The Authority for Discipline

One of the ever-present points of controversy in church discipline is the nature of the church's authority to forgive. Matthew 18:18-20 says:

> Truly, I say to you, whatever you bind on earth shall be bound in heaven, and whatever you loose on earth shall be loosed in heaven.

> Again I say to you, if two of you agree on earth about anything they ask, it will be done for them by my Father in heaven. For where two or three are gathered in my name, there am I in the midst of them.

In this passage, as in John 20:22, 23 and Matthew 16:15-18, it seems unquestionable that in some senses God gives the church the authority to loose or bind, to remit or retain, to forgive or withhold forgiveness of sin. At the same time it seems to many people that the church's claim to possess this authority sounds presumptuous, because the church thereby pretends to usurp the place of God, who alone has authority to forgive sin.

Authority Is Not Autonomy

We must make clear from the outset that the church's authority to bind and loose in discipline is something more than the natural rights usually thought to belong to a social organization. One writer states:

> It belongs to the very nature of a society, and is inherent therein, the power to admit to membership those who profess to act in accordance with its rules, and to exclude those who violate the conditions on which they were admitted. By the nature of its constitutions, as well as in virtue of certain privileges granted by its founder, the church is vested with a similar power.[1]

Another says, "Every institution that has the right to make laws also possesses the right to punish transgressors of these laws."[2]

Gerhard Ebeling gives an effective answer to this misconception. Church discipline, he says,

> must be distinguished from all disciplines and jurisdictions based on human rights. In this sense every human organization protects itself in some fashion or other by a kind of discipline of its members — every union, party, corporation (as for example, a university), every political association, every military organization, and every state. . . . Now church discipline is often enough

> misunderstood and misrepresented in this way
> . . . church discipline is not, however, exercised
> in the name of human justice but through an
> authority delegated to the church by Christ.[3]

Strictly speaking, the church does not possess authority to discipline. It can only be an instrument of the authority of its Lord. In discipline we are therefore dealing with something else than the self-government of an institution. Discipline presupposes subjection of the church to the reign of Christ. That is the presupposition for saying that what is done on earth is done also in heaven.

Confusing church autonomy with Christ's authority is an unfortunately widespread error. People speak of "our church" and "your church" as though it belongs to them, not to God. They assume denominations or conferences have the right to set rules for themselves — conditions of membership, such as the cut of clothes and length of hair. They forget that God sets the conditions of membership in *His* church, and the church's only right is to observe the will of its Lord. In imposing denominational requirements churches today merely repeat the claim of the Medieval Catholic church, in which, as the Reformers said, the pope was usurping the place of the head of the church, Christ.

What then is the right relationship between God and the church in the authority to exercise discipline? An answer to this must begin by clearing away several popular but mistaken notions. The first is that God has committed Himself to ratify the decisions of the church. By this very act of delegating to the church the power of absolution, goes this line of thought, God has bound Himself to endorse in heaven what the church performs upon earth. As one writer expresses it, "Whatever sentence shall be passed and declared by the Governors of the church shall be ratified by Christ whom they represent: which is no more than may be said of the vicegerent of any other prince."[4]

Not Automatic Ratification

But God does not simply automatically ratify every decision in binding and loosing as though He has become a prisoner of the church's arbitrary will. As one theologian says:

> In spite of its being delegated, the authority of church discipline does not cease to remain Christ's authority. It can therefore be exercised only in His name and according to His will.[5]

This implies that there can be acts of discipline not exercised according to Christ's will. Is this not a fateful admission that places a serious question mark over all church discipline? Not necessarily. First, while discipline involves the church in commitment to decisions, these are not at all arbitrary decisions, but attempts by the church to be the executive agency of divine decisions. Second, these decisions are not hidden in inaccessible divine mystery but made known to the church through God's Word and Holy Spirit. The church's reading of such decisions is always subject to review and amendment.

These principles governing the nature of the authority of the church are a warning to the church that it must take its guidance from the Word and Holy Spirit in making its decisions, but they are also a reassurance of its very real and legitimate authority when it does so. In other words, discipline must be based on the gospel, on Christ's requirements for discipleship. When the church begins to usurp the authority of Christ the church merely turns itself into a sect, for then it replaces the requirement of faith with its own doctrine and standards, such as eating fish on Friday or prohibiting buttons in favor of hooks and eyes. A church that does this sooner or later undermines its authority, for men eventually recognize this to be the pretension of a merely human institution, not the authority of Christ through His church.

The apparent presumption of the view that God ratifies the decisions of the church has led some to attempt to reverse the picture and to say that instead of God ratifying the church's decisions the church must ratify God's decisions. Thus one writer argues:

Over half of Christendom believes in sacerdotalism, that is, that certain men have been divinely authorized to forgive sins in behalf of God. And the above passages [John 20:23; Matt. 16:19; 18:18] are the ones quoted to substantiate such a doctrine. My thesis is to prove that the perfect tense has been mistranslated in these passages, and consequently . . . there is no basis for sacerdotalism or priestly absolution in the New Testament.[6]

This writer contends that the passages should be translated, "whatsoever is bound on earth shall have been bound in heaven, and whatsoever is loosed on earth shall have been loosed in heaven." Accordingly, "Jesus warned the disciples that they were to treat as forgiven only those that were already forgiven by God."[7]

The question of "priestly absolution" aside, this interpretation does not hold up exegetically. It falls into contradiction with a text such as Mark 2:5, where the same form of expression is used to describe Jesus' forgiveness of the paralytic. As one critic says in reply to this interpretation: "Luke, like those bystanders, thought that Jesus claimed to forgive sins, not that he treated 'as forgiven only those that were already forgiven by God.' "[8] In this incident God's forgiveness and Jesus' forgiveness of the paralytic are not two separate actions. They are one action, Jesus being the instrument of God's saving work.

For this reason the church has often held this

story before itself as a model of its authority to forgive sin. In the story Jesus says, "The Son of Man has authority on earth to forgive sins," and this authority too is recognized as a new Christian possibility. "The complete identification of the church's and God's judgment is here brought out in its full force. In the church God's judgment is not merely proclaimed, but realized. The church's action is the action of God's presence itself."[9]

The church's decisions in binding and loosing are therefore not just echoes of an action completed by God and then redundantly parroted by the church. Rather, the church, like Christ, is most essential to the process, being united with God as an instrument of His saving work. This point can be seen from other aspects of the texts on binding and loosing. In Matthew 16:18 the promise, "I will give you the keys of the kingdom of heaven," is the context for Jesus' declaration, "On this rock I will build my church." In Matthew 18:19 the promise, "If two of you agree on earth about anything they ask, it will be done for them," has its foundation in the assurance, "For where two or three are gathered in my name, there am I in the midst of them." In John 20:23 the promise, "If you forgive the sins of any, they are forgiven; if you retain the sins of any, they are retained," is based on the words, "As the Father has sent me, even so I send you. . . . Receive the Holy Spirit."

Not Two Churches

Much more common today than the idea that God ratifies the decisions of the church or that the church ratifies the decisions of God is the notion that there is no necessary connection at all between their respective decisions. This notion is usually based on the theory that there is a visible church, held to be the human organization on earth, to be distinguished from the invisible church, the heavenly number of the elect. This view essentially denies the claim that what is bound or loosed on earth is bound or loosed in heaven, for any action the church takes is held to affect only a person's standing in the human institution and does not necessarily touch his status before God. Between the visible church and the invisible church there is no recognizable correlation.

The intention of making the authority of God and that of the church two separate and basically unrelated realms seems to be to avoid the blasphemous claim that God is chained by His own promise of Matthew 18:18, and that the gates of heaven are controlled by an ecclesiastical institution. However, the net effect of this position is to cancel out the significance of the church's decisions, and the further consequence is usually a retreat from definite, specific decisions into the safety of vague generalities.

A good example of this position is Eduard

Thurneysen in his chapter on church discipline in the book, *A Theology of Pastoral Care.* Thurneysen's point of departure is the Heidelberg Catechism, whose question 85 reads, "How is the kingdom of heaven shut and opened by Church Discipline?" The answer in the catechism says:

> If any under the Christian name show themselves unsound either in doctrine or life, and after repeated brotherly admonition refuse to turn from their errors or evil ways, they are complained of to the church or its proper officers, and if they neglect to hear them also, are by them excluded from the Holy Sacraments and the Christian communion, and by God Himself from the kingdom of Christ; and if they promise and show real amendment, they are again received as members of Christ and His church. [10]

This statement is little more than a paraphrase of Matthew 18:15-18, yet Thurneysen thinks it presumptuous that an act of church discipline should actually claim to exclude someone from the kingdom of God. The fact that the Heidelberg Catechism makes room for restoration of those who show "real amendment" Thurneysen construes as an admission that the church does not really believe in its vaunted authority to excommunicate. This restoration, he says,

> causes us to suspect that the refusal of forgiveness, the actual exclusion from the community and Kingdom of Christ, was not meant quite so

171

> seriously after all. If so, we should not threaten
> people with the possibility as if we could effect
> this exclusion by the power of human church
> discipline. It would only be a simulated exclu-
> sion.[11]

But surely the fact that the Heidelberg
Catechism makes room for restoration of the
excommunicated person does not mean the
exclusion from the church was not meant seriously! On the contrary, the act of restoration implies exactly that the exclusion was meant
seriously and was considered valid. What means
the suggestion that "the Gentile and tax collector is primarily and properly the subject of a
new offer of forgiveness,"[12] if the church refuses
seriously to consider him a sinner despite his impenitence?

Those who postulate an invisible church often
quite logically conclude that all the visible
church is authorized to do is proclaim the gospel
in generalities. People who hear this word are
then included or excluded from the kingdom
privately on the basis of their faith or unbelief,
their response directly to God. "The power to
forgive sins or to harden rests in the proclaimed
Word itself," says Thurneysen. "The preacher is
only the servant who communicates the Word,
and as this is done, the unlocking or locking of
the kingdom of heaven is accomplished."[13]

Those who hold this view are consistent, I
hope, and hold the same reservations with re-

gard to baptism. For to baptize implies that it is the rite of baptism (or the withholding of baptism from unbelievers) and not the Word that opens or closes the kingdom of Christ — unless one sees baptism and the Word in the right relationship. Then baptism is recognized as the enacted Word, and hence not in danger of replacing the Word, but becoming its effective operation. Baptism is an operative symbol, "the sign *and* the thing signified." Thus the minister says to the candidate, "I baptize you in the name of the Father, Son, and Holy Spirit," assuming rightly that he is the effective agent of God's working.

May it not be so also with discipline? If discipline is the function of the gospel, may not absolution or excommunication be the enactment of the forgiving or hardening effects of the Word? The problem lies not in discipline, but in the notion that the decisions of discipline in absolution or excommunication should ever be any different than in baptism — the activity of God in and through His church.

It is an equivocation to say simultaneously that discipline is an act of proclaiming the Word and that discipline is rendered superfluous by the Word. If the latter is the case, proclamation of the Word becomes an excuse for not recognizing respective responses to this proclamation — in baptizing or refusing to baptize, absolving or excommunicating. It is God who excludes through the Word, to be sure, but the question remains: who speaks this Word? Surely the church does. How can the church preach that the unrighteous will not inherit the kingdom of God (1 Corinthians 6:9) and yet pretend that it is not called upon to make a decision when confronted by an instance of unrighteousness? It is God indeed who excludes, but His act is performed in the church. Restricting the meaning of binding and loosing to general absolution, as in the Sunday morning liturgy, is an unjustified limitation of its meaning.[14]

We may grant that discipline is a matter of an individual's response to the word of the gospel. Nevertheless the church's responsibility in bringing someone to decision — actually pleading for a decision of faith, but if that is not forthcoming also reluctantly acknowledging the decision of unfaith — cannot be avoided. This process is simply what we mean by discipline. Because of the fear of discipline presuming to be more than the effectual declaration of God's word (which it has been in so much of ecclesiastical history) we must not make it less. That is, the church cannot demur from excluding an impenitent person from the kingdom of Christ, for that would be the surest way of actually excluding him, since by not making known the truth the church would confirm a person in his complacency and self deception

An excellent statement on the point under discussion is given by Lesslie Newbigin in a comment upon 1 Corinthians 5:

> When Paul writes to the Corinthians of the excommunication of the erring brother, it is very clear that he does not say or imply that it is simply a matter of the sinner cutting himself off. He calls for a very solemn and deliberate act of the fellowship — an act in which he himself is completely associated. Moreover, this act is not regarded as merely a severance of external membership, while leaving the man's spiritual relationship with Christ untouched. It is a matter of the most awful meaning — nothing less than delivering him to Satan . . . . To be in the Church's fellowship was to be in Christ, and to be cast out of it was to be delivered over to Satan.[15]

Similarly another theologian, writing out of the missionary situation, maintains that the church's proclamation and warning

> do not come only in the form of general statements. It is the duty of those responsible in the church to address them quite specifically to persons who are plainly living heedless of the claim of Christ. Not only so, but we recognize a solemn authority which the Lord has given to his church actually to exclude from its fellowship any who refuse its warning. Where this authority is reverently exercised in obedience to the Lord's own will, it is stated that the decisions so taken are not of merely earthly significance but concern the eternal destiny of the person concerned.[16]

The nature of the church's authority in discipline may be summed up in the words of Max Thurian on John 20:23:

> This ministry is an aspect of the power of the keys, which ought to be understood as including the whole of the Church's task of setting men free. . . . It is not a question of the ministry of preaching only but of a word and an act which operate what they signify. . . . We have here an example of a sacramental act. . . . The Church believes that God acts conjointly and effectually in a sign which she addresses to the believers. [Sacrament implies] a particular act which entails the action of God himself.[17]

One more point. There are those who seem bothered by the thought that the church would presume to exclude people from the kingdom of God but quite untroubled by the thought that the church presumes to include — in baptism, that is. It should not be overlooked that every act of inclusion itself already implies an exclusion — the exclusion of those not included! Clarence Tucker Craig in a discussion of the general problem of defining the boundaries of the church, which is ultimately what the authority to bind and loose entails, says, "Doubtless we must follow some rough criteria in distinguishing among those who claim to be followers of Christ. But I would much prefer to err on the side of recognizing some whom God does not recognize than excluding those whom he has accepted as his own."[18] We could say just as logically: Why not be strict and let God be gracious in the end, rather than pretending to be more charitable than He and offering false comfort in the process to those for whom this is of ultimate import?

Actually we have more than "rough criteria." As Craig himself says: The "canonical limits" of the church "should extend to the charismatic limits."

> Those who call upon the name of the Lord in faith, who are baptized in his name, have received the Spirit which he gives, and look forward to the consummation of his kingdom — these belong to his body and are the people whom God has called for himself. . . . Wherever the saving grace of God is found, there is the Church.[19]

Exactly. The corollary is that where the saving grace of God is rejected by anyone still claiming membership in God's church, he is to be warned of the fact and, if he remains impenitent, excluded from the church.

Interestingly the modern tendency to accept the church's authority to forgive but to hesitate over its authority to excommunicate is just the opposite of the ancient church's tendency to hold, as Tertullian did, that it can excommunicate but not forgive. Tertullian, as we have noticed, was effectively answered by the Catholic Church. It said that binding and loosing are parallel, as shown in the church's practice of discriminating baptism, which all were obliged to recognize was the exercise of this dual authority.

Let those with an inclination toward lenience note that in Matthew 18 the prescription for discipline ends with the individual as a Gentile and tax collector. And the parable of the unforgiving servant ends with him in prison because of his presumption upon the forgiveness of the king. Of course, acts of excommunication need not be the last word. It is perfectly correct to stress that the Gentile and tax collector is the subject of a new offer of forgiveness. As we have insisted earlier, excommunication does not close the door of the church against the offender's return, though it means that he is not in a state of grace until he returns. Meanwhile, the most promising way of effecting his return is fidelity to the gospel, whose note of judgment is consistent with its basic theme of love.

An understanding of the nature of the church's authority to bind and loose enables us to speak to a second question frequently arising in connection with discipline — namely, the question of church polity. Is the authority to discipline the prerogative of the ministers or is it vested in the whole church as such? From our discussion we have seen that the basic pattern of discipline is the authority of God over the church. This must not be compromised or distorted in any fashion by another pattern such as the authority of the ministers over the laity. The church is the body of Christ, not the body of the ministers. Accordingly church discipline should never be permitted to degenerate into discipline of the laity by the clergy. It is discipline of members by the body under the authority of Christ.

This view is nothing more than an implication of the doctrine of the priesthood of all believers. There may be some persons in the church (not necessarily ministers) who are recognized as having the gift of admonition and counsel. Anyone, however, is free to go to a brother with the word of admonition, just as anyone is free to speak the word of witness on behalf of the church in evangelism. As a member of the body of Christ he is already a representative of the church and thus under the authority of Christ. Also there is no special "confessor" to whom every sinner must go, an individual who alone is qualified to hear confession and confer absolution.

To deny that the exercise of disciplinary authority is the prerogative of the clergy does not call in question the place of an ordered ministry. When discipline involves the act of excommunication or restoration, it takes place on the level of the whole congregation. It is at this congregational level of action that it is entirely appropriate and even necessary for the matter to be handled by duly ordained officers of the church. Ministers are involved in the task of discipline just as they are for the conduct of worship, for teaching, for celebration of the sacraments, and for the administration of other aspects of church life. And this parallel shows, incidentally, that this task should fall to congregational ministers and not to nonresident bishops.

But the handling of this matter is done by the ministers as ministers of the congregation. The action is ultimately congregational action under Christ, not the action of a minister in independence of the congregation. The reason is that the church as such, the whole people of God, stands under the authority of Christ and is His agent in the task of discipline — as it is also in the task of missionary proclamation.

9

YOU

WHO ARE SPIRITUAL
Getting on with the Task

I think it is safe to say that the recovery of a healthy church discipline will not be easy. As mentioned at the outset, the church is afflicted with a kind of paralysis resulting from an inner ambivalence — a desire to observe biblical precept countered by a fear of repeating the blunders of the past. This book has attempted to remove some of these fears and thus clear the way in the church for obedience to the teaching of Jesus.

In the preceding pages we have tried to show that congregational discipline is the act of discipling the brother. According to Matthew 18 the act of going to the brother is a function of the gospel analogous to evangelism or missionary proclamation. In discipline, as in the presentation of the good news to a non-Christian, a person is presented the opportunity of being liberated from the power of sin in all its forms by coming under the rule of Christ and walking in His way.

What is at stake is nothing less than the life of the church itself. This is not intended simply as shocking rhetoric. It has become an accepted article of recent theology to consider evangelism as part of the essence of the life of the church and not merely a desirable but ultimately optional ideal. In Brunner's well-known words, "The church exists by mission as fire exists by burning." Unfortunately congregational discipline has not yet been granted that position, although according to Reformation thought church discipline was one of the marks of the church.

Congregational discipline belongs to the essence of the church as much as evangelism because both are inescapable implications of the gospel. It makes no sense to declare the good news of liberation from sin to people outside the church and then refuse to declare it to Christians within the church. The gospel is not merely good news by which the sinner can be converted. It is also good news by which the Christian can continue to live.

Not just on the basis of theological principle, but in practice also, it makes no sense to accept the task of evangelism and then to neglect discipline. What is the point of adding people to the church through gospel proclamation if membership in that church becomes meaningless because of a failure of discipline? Evangelism itself is soon undermined if people discover that in the absence of discipline to belong or not to belong to the church really makes no difference.

If there is aggressive evangelism without supporting discipline in the church created by that evangelism, there comes a shift in the purpose of the evangelistic program. It often ceases to be considered the task of incorporating people into a church and becomes instead a religious experience for its own sake. We see this sort of thing in modern revivalism when people — most of them already members of the church — go through periodic "conversions" which carry little meaning beyond a temporary emotional charge. After all, if persons are already members of a church, what else could conversion mean?

There are some who might still ask, however, Isn't modern revivalism consistent with the thesis that congregational discipline is a function of the gospel? The answer is that much modern revivalism fails to take seriously the most basic thing envisaged by the gospel, namely, the church. Proclaiming the gospel means calling people into that community which accepts the rule of God and lives for its eventual full realization on earth.

It is clear, then, that congregational discipline is of primary importance. Without it the church ceases to have meaning, and without a meaningful church, evangelism also loses its meaning. It is mistaken to think, therefore, as some modern popular theology seems to hold, that ever more aggressive evangelism will make up for the neglect of discipline and its consequent weakening of the church. Ever bigger and better crusades will not solve the problem of sin in the church. The more worldly the church, the more danger of big crusades becoming a farce. The call for more evangelism not backed by discipleship ends up as "cheap grace."

The parallel we have shown between gospel proclamation and congregational discipline implies that both are equally indispensable to the realization of the kingdom of God. In the light of this we can insist that the recovery of discipline according to the gospel will strengthen the mission of the church. Evangelism will be clarified when people see that conversion leads to a discipled life in the church. The outreach of the church can only benefit from faithful discipline.

No doubt some people will think that an attempt to recover this ministry of discipling the brother will lead back to the kind of legalism that has characterized so much of the history of the church. This can happen, of course, but only if discipline ceases to ground itself in the gospel. As we have seen, the alternatives are not legalism or indulgence. It is therefore not acceptable to pit one against the other and to say that indulgence is no worse than legalism. When laxity is put forward as the answer to legalism, it shows that people have not yet caught sight of the gospel. The real options are the liberation of people through the gospel or their continued bondage to sin in the form of either indulgence or legalism. Neither legalism nor indulgence provides persons with true liberation from sin.

A recovery of discipline does not therefore imply a new era of the inquisition. There are, frankly, problems to be faced in churches where discipline has been neglected and a backlog of sin in the church has been allowed to build up. Where congregational discipline is exercised properly, however, its effect is to reduce the number of instances of corrective discipline that arise because the meaning of discipleship is kept clearly in view. It is just like discipline in a home, says one writer. "We may say of a Christian congregation that it is well disciplined, not when perpetually engaged in efforts to reclaim offenders, but when there are few offenders to be reclaimed."[1] Instances of discipline are not, of course, to be desired. But if sin makes its appearance, discipline is very much to be desired as the answer to the problem.

Too many people think that congregational discipline is somehow a disgrace to the church, and therefore cases of discipline are swept under the rug. The really serious disgrace, however, is failure to tender help to a stumbling brother. What is disgraceful about offering a thief, let's say, liberation from compulsions that are robbing him of a life of genuine happiness, the kind of life God intends for him? And if he refuses such liberation, what is disgraceful about reminding him honestly that such conduct is incompatible with life in the kingdom of God? Such integrity becomes at this stage the only avenue to his liberation.

Congregational discipline will not be considered a disgrace if it is carried out redemptively instead of punitively. Recall that Jesus' invitation to tax collectors and sinners was an attempt to reclaim people excommunicated from the synagogue. Surely His call to discipleship is not to be considered an embarrassment or disgrace! On the contrary, it issues in joy and celebration, as we see from the parable of the prodigal son. That is what it can and should be in our churches too.

Identifying the Task

"Brethren, if a man is overtaken in any trespass, you who are spiritual should restore him in a spirit of gentleness. Look to yourself, lest you too be tempted. Bear one another's burdens, and so fulfill the law of Christ," writes Paul (Gal. 6:1, 2).

We can summarize under six headings what we have said in the foregoing chapters about the task of discipling.

(1) *The church is a spiritual body.* It is launched by the coming of the Spirit at Pentecost, and receiving the life of the Spirit is the condition of membership. Hence baptism should coincide with the recognition of the regenerating work of the Spirit. We call this a believers' church.

(2) *The process of discipling should be initiated where the church notices signs of faltering spiritual life.* We sometimes think that where nothing happens in a Christian's life, he is alright. Only if an act of sin appears is something wrong. Actually it's the other way around. Where the signs of spiritual life are apparent, there is healthy Christian life. If these signs disappear, something is wrong. Then others in the church should come with help.

(3) *The goal of discipling is the recovery of spiritual life.* The church can fall into the mistake of seeking other objectives, usually an outward social respectability that is not generated by the renewing work of God's Spirit in the "inner man." Often punishment is the method resorted to, because it is an external constraint calculated to elicit the desired conduct. But it cannot change a person's nature. Only the Spirit can do that.

(4) *Given the foregoing conditions, it follows that the work of discipling can be accomplished only by spiritual people.* That is why Paul in the text quoted above addresses himself to those who are spiritual. Sometimes we think that to be spiritual means not to come into contact with evil. But spiritual people should want to help someone in

trouble, since it is the nature of spiritual life to love and help.

(5) *If discipling is done by spiritual people for a spiritual goal, we should expect it to be carried out in a spiritual way.* Paul calls it the spirit of gentleness and humility. If we stop to think about the relationship of means and end, it is absurd to expect cold, harsh measures to achieve repentance and faith. That is why Paul asks the spiritual to examine themselves, for that is the only way to bring another person to examine himself.

(6) *The outcome of efforts at disicpling must be judged by spiritual criteria.* Where a person lets the power of the Spirit transform his life he of course continues in the spiritual body, the church. But if he shuts out the Spirit, he alas shuts himself out of the community of the Spirit, and this evenuality must then be recognized honestly for what it is.

Practical First Steps

You may have heard of the Irishman who was asked for directions by a traveler and replied, "You can't start from here." Many churches see the need of instituting a ministry of discipling the faltering Christian but believe they can't start from where they are because their church is no longer a spiritual body. And that seems to be the prerequisite according to Galatians 6:1, 2. Consider the following suggested steps:

(1) *Begin with a study of the meaning of Christian life.* Such a task will be difficult because we

must go beyond the shallow definitions and stereotypes we are sometimes offered. We must not, however, define spiritual life in terms of an increased number of commandments. Rather we must sharpen our spiritual sensibility to get a feel for the spirit of life in Christ as portrayed in the Sermon on the Mount.

(2) *Review the membership of your congregation or fellowship.* Such an undertaking might be called a covenant renewal, which begins with each member examining himself to see whether he possesses living faith (2 Cor. 13:5). But it will also have to go beyond this to review the actual membership in your congregation. Are there absentee members? Are there members with no signs of spiritual life? Begin by identifying obvious inconsistencies in an effort to make the membership of your congregation coincide with life in the Spirit.

(3) *Establish a congregational policy for discipling.* That means in the first place establishing a climate of trust and mutual aid, establishing the understanding that concern and counsel are not a matter of prying into someone's life but our desire to see each other grow in grace and in the knowledge of Jesus Christ.

It means in the second place establishing quite specific and practical lines of responsibility so that it doesn't take a year before someone notices that a certain individual has not been showing up in church anymore. Have an understanding of how a church member can proceed if he senses that another member is faltering in his spiritual life.

The ministry of discipling an erring fellow Christian where this becomes needed must be accepted as part of normal church life in the same way that initial witness and discipling are seen as the ongoing task of the church.

(4) *Take the next case of a need for discipling that arises and carry it through with all the love, sensitiveness, and honesty that you know.* Refuse to make excuses out of past neglect or mistakes. If we make mistakes, then, as in evangelism, we can try to make these right and learn from such experiences to do better next time. We want people to inherit all the power, love, joy, peace, freedom, righteousness, hope, and life in the Spirit that God offers His human creation.

FOOTNOTES

CHAPTER 1

1. Geddes MacGregor, *The Coming Reformation* (Philadelphia: The Westminster Press, 1960), p. 17.

2. Alan Richardson, article "Devote" in *A Theological Word Book of the Bible* (New York: The Macmillan Company, 1956), p. 68.

3. Rudolf Bohren, *Das Problem der Kirchenzucht im neuen Testament* (Zollikon-Zürich: Evangelischer Verlag, 1952), p. 25.

4. For further information on Jewish discipline see relevant articles such as those under "Ban" and "Excommunication" in *The Jewish Encyclopedia* (1903) and *The Universal Jewish Encyclopedia* (1941).

5. R. H. Charles (ed.), *The Apocrypha and Pseudepigrapha*, Vol. II: *Pseudepigrapha* (Oxford: At the Claredon Press, 1913), pp. 341, 342.

6. S. L. Greenslade, *Shepherding the Flock* (London: SCM Press, Ltd., 1967), p. 92.

7. Bohren, *op. cit.*, p. 13.

8. According to Oscar D. Watkins, *A History of Penance* (London: Longmans, Green & Co., 1920), vol. 1, p. 472.

9. Nathaniel Marshall, *The Penitential Doctrine of the Primitive Church* (Oxford: John Henry Parker, 1714, 1844), pp. 50, 51. Brackets Marshall's.

10. R. S. T. Haslehurst, *Some Account of the Penitential Discipline of the Early Church in the First Four Centuries* (London: SPCK, 1921), p. 87.

11. Watkins, *op. cit.*, p. 472.

12. Marshall, *op. cit.*, p. 53. Brackets Marshall's.

13. *Ibid.*, p. 180.

14. Philip Schaff, *History of the Christian Church*, Vol. II (Grand Rapids: Wm. B. Eerdmans Publishing Company, 1950), p. 189.

15. Watkins, *op. cit.*, Vol. II, p. 755.

16. *Ibid.*, pp. 755, 756. See also Henry Charles Lea, *A History of Auricular Confession and Indulgences in the Latin Church* (Philadelphia: Lea Brothers & Co., 1896) and an introduction to the medieval penitentials in John T. McNeill and Helena M. Gamer, *Medieval Handbooks of Penance* (New York: Columbia University Press, 1938).

17. Watkins, *op cit.*, p. 755.

18. *Ibid.*, p. 759.

19. *Ibid.*, p. 768.

20. Alexis Aurelius Pelliccia, *The Polity of the Christian Church of Early, Medieval, and Modern Times*, trans. J. C. Bellett (London: J. Masters & Co., 1883), p. 442.

21. Lea, *op. cit.*, Vol. 1, pp. 36, 37.

22. Roger Ley, *Kirchenzucht bei Zwingli* (Zürich: Zwingli Verlag, 1948), p. 6.

23. Wilhelm Maurer, *Gemeindezucht, Gemeindeamt, Konfirmation* ("Schriftenreihe des Pfarrervereins Kurhessen — Waldeck," Heft 2, Herausgeber Pfarrer Dr. Hans Schimmelfeng; Im Johannes Stauda-Verlag zu Kassel, 1940), p. 9.

24. Ruth Götze, *Wie Luther Kirchenzucht Ubte* (Göttingen: Vandenhoeck & Ruprecht, 1958), pp. 128, 129.

25. Article "Kirchenzucht" in *Realencyclopädie für protestantische Theologie und Kirche*, Vol. X (1901).

26. Noted by William Klassen, *The Forgiving Community* (Philadelphia: The Westminster Press, 1966), p. 180.

27. See article "Church Discipline" in *The New Schaff-Herzog Encyclopedia* (1952).

28. Article "Kirchenzucht" in the 1912 edition of *Religion in Geschichte und Gegenwart*.

29. Article "Kirchenzucht" in *Realencyklopädie*.

30. "Church Discipline" in *The New Schaff-Herzog Encyclopedia*.

31. Quoted from Eduard Thurneysen, *A Theology of Pastoral Care*, trans. Jack A. Worthington and Thomas Wieser (Richmond: John Knox Press, 1962), pp. 32, 33.

32. Article "Discipline" in Hastings, *Encyclopedia of Religion and Ethics*.

33. Edited by J. C. Wenger, *The Mennonite Quarterly Review*, XIX (1945), pp. 244-253.

34. Menno Simons, *The Complete Writings*, trans. Leonard Verduin, ed. J. C. Wenger (Scottdale: Herald Press, 1956).

35. David J. Markey, "An Inquiry into the Life and Teaching of Alexander Mack with Special Reference to His View of Church Discipline" (unpublished MA thesis, Northwestern University, 1954).

36. Article "Church Discipline" in Hastings, *Encyclopedia of Religion and Ethics*.

37. According to Geddes MacGregor, *Corpus Christi* (Philadelphia: The Westminster Press, 1958), p. 105.

38. A comprehensive account of church discipline among the New England Puritans is Emil Oberholzer, Jr., *Delinquent Saints* (New York: Columbia University Press, 1956), a study of all church discipline cases up to about 1830 found in the available records of those

Massachusetts Puritan Churches founded before 1765.

39. See Frederick Norwood, *Church Membership in the Methodist Tradition* (Nashville: The Methodist Publishing House, 1958).

40. See article "Kirchenzucht" in *Religion in Geschichte und Gegenwart* (1959).

41. Hans Dürr, "Kirchenzucht in den Missionskirchen-und bei uns?" in *Festschrift fur D. Albert Schädelin*, Herausgeber Hans Dürr (Bern: Verlag Herbert Lang & Cie, 1950), pp. 156-162.

42. Lesslie Newbigin, *The Household of God* (New York: Association Press, 1954), p. 7.

43. Emil Brunner, *The Divine Imperative* (Philadelphia: The Westminster Press, 1947), pp. 558, 559.

44. Gerhard Ebeling, *Kirchenzucht* (Stuttgart: W. Kohlhammer Verlag, 1947), p. 10.

45. F. John Taylor, *The Church of God* (London: The Canterbury Press, 1946), p. 156.

46. To the list of books already mentioned we would add James Leo Garrett, *Baptist Church Discipline* (Nashville: Broadman Press, 1962) and Donald Bloesch, *The Reform of the Church* (Grand Rapids: Wm. B. Eerdmans Publishing Company, 1970).

CHAPTER 2

1. Quoted by Thurneysen, *op. cit.*, p. 47.

2. *Institutes*, Book 4, XI, 1.

3. *Op. cit.*, p. 989.

4. *Loc. cit.*

5. Alfred Plummer, *An Exegetical Commentary on the Gospel According to St. Matthew* (London: Robert Scott, 1909), p. 229.

6. William Barclay, *The Gospel of Matthew* (Philadelphia: The Westminster Press, 1958), Vol. II, pp. 154, 155.

7. Oscar Cullmann, *Peter: Disciple, Apostle, Martyr*, trans. Floyd V. Filson (New York: Meridian Books, Inc., 1958), pp. 184-212.

8. Wilhelm Vischer, *Die Evangelische Gemeindeordnung, Matthaus* 16:13 — 20:28 (Zollikon-Zürich: Evangelischer Verlag, 1946), p. 17.

9. Eduard Schweizer, *Church Order in the New Testament*, trans. Frank Clarke ("Studies in Biblical Theology"; London: SCM Press, Ltd., 1961), p. 59.

10. Geddes MacGregor, *Corpus Christi*, pp. 103, 104.

11. Barclay, *op. cit.*, pp. 206, 207.

CHAPTER 3

1. Roger Ley, *op. cit.*, p. 14.

2. Max Thurian, *Confession* (London: SCM Press, Ltd., 1958), p. 43.

3. Bohren, *op. cit.*, pp. 49, 50.

4. Roger Ley shows what deplorable consequences followed from Zwingli's policing system initiated by the March 26, 1530, mandate, one of them being the loss of trust in pastors, who were forced into the role of prosecutors. *Op. cit.*, p. 121.

5. Garrett, *op cit.*, p. 42.

6. Heinz Daniel Janzen, "*Anabaptist Church Discipline in the Light of the New Testament*" (unpublished BD thesis, Biblical Seminary, New York, 1956), p. 26.

7. Menno Simons' classification, according to Frank C. Peters, "The Ban in the Writings and Life of Menno Simons" (unpublished MA thesis, Toronto Graduate School of Theological Studies and Emmanuel College, 1953), p. 56. Menno's primary categories, however, are "falling" into sin and remaining in error. Persons in the former are to be repeatedly admonished, as necessary; only those in the latter are to be excommunicated.

8. Herbert Henley Henson, *Moral Discipline in the Christian Church* (London: Longmans, Green & Co., 1905), p. 60.

9. Lea, *op. cit.*, Vol. I, p. 35.

10. Marshall, *op. cit.*, p. 197.

11. From Warwick Elwin, *Confession and Absolution in the Bible* (London: J. T. Hayes, 1883), p. 4. Pelliccia describes how the three classes of sins were matched by "three different kinds of punishment which the church used to inflict on offenders," *op. cit.*, p. 417.

12. Lea, *op. cit.*, Vol. II, p. 162.

13. Haslehurst, *op. cit.*, p. 32.

14. Quoted in Haslehurst, *ibid.*, p. 36.

15. Bohren, *op. cit.*, pp. 86-91.

16. The suggestion of the possibility of a fall from grace may not be palatable to Calvinists who insist upon a rigid doctrine of the perseverance of the saints. If one does not allow the possibility of a fall from grace, the incidence of sin in the church and eventual excommunication for it must be construed as the exposure of a hypocrite, and that in turn will likely be explained in terms of an "invisible" church (i.e., promiscuous membership in the visible church).

We cannot go into a discussion of this issue here. It is enough to say that in the actual practice of discipline the issue is not important. If an impenitent sinner is excluded from the church, whether as an exposed hypocrite or as one who falls from grace, the church's ground for this course of action remains the same — recognition of that sinner's rejection of the grace proffered him in the gospel.

CHAPTER 4

1. Marshall, *op, cit.*, pp. 50, 51.

2. Janzen, *op. cit.*, p. 66.

3. *Op. cit.*, pp. 974 ff.

4. Williston Walker, *The Creeds and Platforms of Congregationalism* (Boston: The Pilgrim Press, 1960), p. 228.

5. In American Puritanism discipline was usually initiated by a charge filed against some individual for having broken the fourth, seventh, or tenth commandment. Oberholzer, *op. cit., passim.*

6. Karl Barth, *The Faith of the Church*, ed. Jean-Louis Leuba, trans. Gabriel Vahanian (New York: Meridian Books, Inc., 1958), pp. 157, 158.

CHAPTER 5

1. Ley, *op. cit.*, p. 128.

2. E. Tyrrell Green, *The Church of Christ, Her Mission, Sacraments, and Discipline* (London: Methuen & Co., 1902), p. 339.

3. I would hesitate to accept Luther's statement that gamblers, revelers, drunkards, libertines, blasphemers, and mockers need not be banned, since they ban themselves by not going to Word and sacrament. (Luther adds that a pastor is to deny such persons all Christian ordinances from baptism to burial.) Götze, *op. cit.*, pp. 14, 15. Since there is not room for two levels of church membership — communing and communionless — the church must through admonition bring such people to faithful reception of communion or else endorse their rejection of grace by formal excommunication.

4. Pelliccia, *op. cit.*, pp. 484, 485. Such a distinction was not known until the age of Gratian, says Pelliccia.

5. Article "Excommunication," *The Catholic Encyclopedia* (1913).

6. *The Book of Concord*, trans. and ed. by Theodore G. Tappert (Philadelphia: Muhlenberg Press, 1959), p. 314.

7. Leon Morris, *The First Epistle of Paul to the Corinthians* (Wm. B. Eerdmans Publishing Company, 1958), p. 88. This view is also taken by the *Interpreter's Bible*.

8. Thurian, *op. cit.*, p. 46.

9. Edwin Lowell Adams, "A Study of Corrective Discipline in

the Apostolic Church" (unpublished doctoral dissertation, Southern Baptist Theological Seminary, Louisville, Kentucky, 1949), pp. 194, 195.

10. Robertson and Plummer draw attention to Paul's use of *sarx* instead of *soma* in 1 Corinthians 5:5. In Rom. 6:6, however, *soma* is used. This inconsistency does not invalidate our point. If destruction of the "sinful body" does not denote physical suffering, "destruction of the flesh" is even less likely to, since *sarx* is the more characteristic Pauline expression for man's sinful nature. See Archibald Robertson and Alfred Plummer, *First Epistle of St. Paul to the Corinthians* (New York: Charles Scribner's Sons, 1916), p. 99.

11. Thurian, *op. cit.*, p. 46.

12. Thomas Witherow, *The Form of the Christian Temple* (Edinburgh: T. & T. Clark, 1889), p. 153.

13. Walker, *op. cit.*, p. 39.

14. Article "Anathema" in *The Catholic Encyclopedia.*

15. Götze, *op. cit.*, pp. 118, 119.

16. *Institutes*, Book 4, XII, 10.

17. Haslehurst, *op. cit.*, p. 22.

18. Jean Lasserre, *War and the Gospel*, trans. Oliver Coburn (Scottdale: Herald Press, 1962), pp. 50, 51.

CHAPTER 6

1. Haslehurst, *op. cit.*, p. 26.

2. Walker, *op. cit.*, p. 39.

3. Peters, *op. cit.*, p. 62, quoting Menno. On the practical application of his general rule Menno vacillated, and hesitated to go along with the "hard" banners. On the one hand he held that the ban has no respect for persons, but on the other hand he said marital avoidance could not be forced upon people. He did write that shunning was in no way a temporary dissolution of the marriage. *Ibid.*, pp. 97-99. In a Strassbourg meeting of 1557 fifty bishops from Alsace, Switzerland, Baden, Würtemberg, and Moravia discussed shunning and rejected the severe position of Menno (as they understood it), and made clear that the command concerning marriage overrides that of the ban (meaning avoidance). Menno replied to the Strassbourg gesture in 1558 with "A Fundamental Doctrine . . ." in which "he expounded the ban in its strictest measures." Bauman reports that in early Dutch Mennonitism couples were interrogated at their wedding in the presence of the congregation as to their willingness to shun their spouse in

case one should fall under the ban, and an affirmative answer was required. Irwin W. Bauman, "The Early Development of the Ban and Avoidance in the Mennonite Church" (unpublished BD thesis, Hartford Theological Seminary, 1926), p. 74.

4. Markey, *op. cit.*, pp. 94, 95.

5. Marshall, *op. cit.*, p. 53.

6. *Ibid.*, Appendix I.

7. *Ibid.*

8. Haslehurst, *op. cit.*, p. 117.

9. Elwin, *op. cit.*, pp. 316, 317. Beecher confirms this; he notes that a catechumen could not do penance because he was not a member of the church. Lyman Beecher, *The Antiquities of the Christian Church* (Andover: Gould, Newman and Saxton, 1841), p. 331. Marshall notes the discrimination. "When the party excommunicated was softened into submission, he was longer than in recovering the privileges he had forfeited, than he was at first in gaining them; nor could he be readmitted to communion upon terms so easy as those upon which he was first admitted to it. And, therefore, the penitent passed through more stages, and was longer detained from communion, than the catechumen." Marshall, *op. cit.*, pp. 49, 50.

10. Watkins, *op. cit.*, Vol. I, p. 182.

CHAPTER 7

1. Quoted in Archibald Hunter, *Interpreting the Parables* (Philadelphia: The Westminster Press, 1960), p. 33.

2. Joachim Jeremias, *The Parables of Jesus* (New York: Charles Scribner's Sons, 1955), p. 157.

3. Noted by Jeremias, *ibid.*, and Hunter, *op. cit.*, p. 46.

4. Clarence Tucker Craig, for example, balances them against each other in *The One Church* (Nashville: Abingdon Cokesbury Press, 1951), p. 37.

5. Bohren, *op. cit.*, p. 56.

6. Götze, *op. cit.*, p. 126.

7. Ley, *op. cit.*, p. 33.

8. William Palmer, *A Treatise on the Church of Christ* (London: J. G. F. & J. Rivington, 1842), Vol. I, p. 228.

9. Jonathan Edwards, *Works* (Worcester: Isaiah Thomas, Jr., 1808), Vol. I, p. 289.

10. *Op. cit.*, p. 46.

11. *Op. cit.*, p. 155.

12. Hunter, *op. cit.*, p. 45.

13. C. H. Dodd, *The Parables of the Kingdom* (Glasgow: Collins, 1961), pp. 138, 139.

14. *Ibid.*

15. *Op. cit.*, p. 155.

16. *Op. cit.*, pp. 140, 141.

17. *Op. cit.*, pp. 56-58. Bohren refers in this connection to Paul's remark in 1 Cor. 5:12, "For what have I to do with judging outsiders?"

18. Walter Hobhouse, *The Church and the World in Idea and in History* (London: Macmillan and Co., Ltd., 1910), pp. 395, 396.

19. *Op. cit.*, p. 605. Perhaps Trench had a point when he commented upon the parable thus: "By this prohibition (of uprooting) are forbidden all such measures for the excision of heretics, as shall leave them no room for after repentance or amendment; indeed, the prohibition is so clear, so express, that whenever we meet in Church history with ought which looks like a carrying out of this proposal, we may be tolerably sure that it is not wheat making war on tares, but tares seeking to root out wheat." Richard Chevenix Trench, *Notes on the Parables of Our Lord* (New York: Fleming H. Revell Company, n.d.), pp. 80, 81.

20. *Luther's Meditations on the Gospels,* trans. and arranged by Roland H. Bainton (Philadelphia: The Westminster Press, 1962), p. 74. The not uncommon thought that one should hesitate to uproot the tares because they might become wheat (which Luther mentions first) is not really the point of the parable, but comes closer to the spirit of it than do many other interpretations.

21. Lea, *op. cit.*, Vol. II, p. 162.

22. Emil Brunner, *Dogmatics.* Vol. III: *The Christian Doctrine of the Church, Faith and the Consummation* (Philadelphia: The Westminster Press, 1962), pp. 28, 29.

23. *Op. cit.*, p. 19.

24. *Ibid.*, pp. 31-45.

25. Quoted in John D. Godsey, *The Theology of Dietrich Bonhoeffer* (Philadelphia: Westminster Press, 1960), p. 49. Is Bonhoeffer's theory of worldly Christianity, developed toward the end of his life, an attempt to get away from these invalid distinctions? In *The Cost of Discipleship* Bonhoeffer, commenting on the Sermon on the Mount, remarks: "Flight into the invisible is a denial of the call. A community of Jesus which seeks to hide itself has ceased to follow him. 'Neither do men light a lamp and put it under a bushel, but on the stand.' . . . The light may be covered of its own choice. . . . But the motive may be more sinister than that; it may be 'Reformation theology' which boldly claims the name of *theologia crucis*, and pretends to prefer to Pharisaic ostentation a

modest invisibility, which in practice means conformity to the world. When that happens . . . the very failure of the light to shine becomes the touchstone of our Christianity." Dietrich Bonhoeffer, *The Cost of Discipleship*, trans. Reginald H. Fuller (New York: The Macmillan Company, 1963), pp. 132, 133.

26. Quoted in Norwood, *op. cit.*, p. 74.

CHAPTER 8

1. Witherow, *op. cit.*, p. 147.

2. Ferdinand Probst, *Kirchliche Disciplin in den drei ersten christlichen Jahrhunderten* (Tübingen: Verlag der H. Lauppschen Buchhandlung, 1873), p. 385.

3. *Op. cit.*, pp. 53-55.

4. John Potter, *A Discourse of Church Government* (Philadelphia: S. Potter & Co., 1824), p. 304.

5. Ebeling, *op. cit.*, p. 56.

6. J. R. Mantey, "The Mistranslation of the Perfect Tense in John 20:23, Matthew 16:19 and Matthew 18:18, "*Journal of Biblical Literature*, vol. 58, 1939, pp. 243-249. Howard in the *Interpreter's Bible* also notes the periphrastic future perfect in this text, claiming it "implies insight into a granting or withholding of forgiveness already determined in the divine judgment." Vol. VIII, p. 798.

7. *Op. cit.*

8. Henry J. Cadbury, "The Meaning of John 20:23, Matthew 16:19, and Matthew 18:18," *Journal of Biblical Literature*, vol. 58, 1939, pp. 251-254.

9. Hans Freiherr von Campenhausen, *Kirchliches Amt und geistliche Vollmacht in den ersten drei Jahrhunderten* (Tübingen: J. C. B. Mohr [Paul Siebeck], 1953), p. 137.

10. *Op. cit.*, pp. 44 ff.

11. *Ibid.*, p. 47.

12. *Ibid.*, pp. 46, 47.

13. *Ibid.*, p. 48.

14. Campenhausen, *op. cit.*, p. 153.

15. Newbigin, *op. cit.*, p. 55.

16. William Stewart, *The Nature and Calling of the Church* (Mysore: The Christian Literature Society, 1958), p. 77.

17. *Op. cit.*, pp. 51, 52. We would prefer "mediates" to "entails."

18. *Op. cit.*, p. 34.

19. *Ibid.*, pp. 34, 42.

CHAPTER 9

1. Warham Walker, *Church Discipline* (Boston: Gould, Kendall & Lincoln, 1844), p. 24.

SELECTED BIBLIOGRAPHY

Bloesch, Donald G. *The Reform of the Church*. Grand Rapids: The Wm. B. Eerdmans Publishing Company, 1970. One chapter calling for a recovery of discipline as part of a contemporary reform of the church.

Bohren, Rudolf. *Das Problem der Kirchenzucht im neuen Testament*. Zollikon-Zürich: Evangelischer Verlag, 1952. Good theological analysis but very Calvinist view on the perseverance of the saints.

Concern No. 14. A Pamphlet Series for Questions of Christian Renewal (Scottdale: Concern, 1967).

Garrett, James Leo. *Baptist Church Discipline*. Nashville: Broadman Press, 1962. Introduction to and reprint of an early American Baptist discipline.

Götze, Ruth. *Wie Luther Kirchenzucht Ubte*. Göttingen: Vandenhoeck & Ruprecht, 1958. A review of Luther's record which faces up to his mistakes but cannot question the source of those mistakes in his two-kingdom theology.

Greenslade, S. L. *Shepherding the Flock*, London: SCM Press, Ltd., 1967. A missionary reviewing early church discipline and suggesting possible applications in today's younger churches.

Haslehurst, R. S. T. *Some Account of the Penitential Discipline of the Early Church in the First Four Centuries*. London: SPCK, 1921. Good survey.

Klassen, William. *The Forgiving Community*. Philadelphia: The Westminster Press, 1966. A chapter on the need of discipline as pedagogy in the forgiving community, the church.

Ley, Roger. *Kirchenzucht bei Zwingli*. Zürich: Zwingli Verlag, 1948. Criticism and defense of this reformer's discipline theory and practice.

MacGregor, Geddes. *The Coming Reformation*. Philadelphia: The Westminster Press, 1960. A chapter arguing the need for the Reformed tradition to recover discipline.

Marshall, Nathaniel. *The Penitential Doctrine of the Primitive Church*. Oxford: John Henry Parker, 1844 reprint of 1714 edition. An Anglican commends the early church for its firm discipline and advocates bringing some of it into the Anglican Church.

Menno Simons. *The Complete Writings*. Translated by Leonard Verduin. Edited by J. C. Wenger. Scottdale: Herald Press, 1956. Contains three essays on Menno's considered position. In the second and third a beleaguered Menno is in polemic with the "hard banners."

Norwood, Frederick. *Church Membership in the Methodist Tradition*. Nashville: The Methodist Publishing House, 1958. "Getting in and putting out" in the Methodist tradition.

Oberholzer, Emil, Jr. *Delinquent Saints*. New York: Columbia University Press, 1956. A review of discipline in New England Puritanism which is not too sympathetic because it tends to follow the stereotype of Puritanism.

Rowdon, H. H. "Puritan Church Discipline." Annual Public Lecture. London: London Bible College, [1960]. A pamphlet urging the recovery of church discipline in modern evangelicalism.

Shelly, Maynard (ed.). *Studies in Church Discipline*. Newton: Mennonite Publication Office, 1958. Essays on problems of discipline in today's church. Tends toward the practical rather than the theological.

Stewart, Wm. *The Nature and Calling of the Church*. Mysore: The Christian Literature Society, 1958. Contains a good chapter on the need for discipline by a churchman in the younger church.

Taylor, F. John. *The Church of God*. London: The Canterbury Press, 1946. Also contains a chapter on the need for church discipline today.

Thurian, Max. *Confession*. London: SCM Press, Ltd., 1958. A theologian from a French Protestant monastic community feels total rejection of Catholic confession forfeits some basic Christian values.

Thurneysen, Eduard. *A Theology of Pastoral Care*. Trans. by Jack A. Worthington and Thomas Wieser. Richmond: John Knox Press, 1962. Swiss neoorthodox theologian and friend of Barth has a chapter on the importance of discipline, but refuses to give it any more significance than the formal proclamation of the Word.

Walker, Warham. *Church Discipline*. Boston: Gould, Kendall & Lincoln, 1844. A remarkably perceptive and comprehensive theological statement of the doctrine of church discipline.

Watkins, Oscar D. *A History of Penance*. 2 vols. London: Longmans, Green & Co., 1920. Thorough survey of the subject indicated in the title.

Marlin Jeschke was born near Waldheim, Sask. He attended Prairie Bible Institute, Three Hills, Alta., and received his BA from Tabor College, Hillsboro, Kan. He attended Goshen Biblical Seminary, Goshen, Ind., for one semester. He received his BD from Garrett Theological Seminary, and his PhD in theology from Northwestern University, both in Evanston, Ill.

He taught for two years part-time at North Park College, Chicago, and joined the Goshen College faculty in 1961. In 1968-69 he took a leave of absence under a fellowship in Asian religions to study at the Harvard Center for World Religions for five months and to travel for six months in Muslim and Buddhist areas of the Middle East, South-East Asia, and Japan. He is presently professor of philosophy and religion at Goshen College.

He was baptized at the age of eighteen into a Mennonite Church at Waldheim, Sask. For five years he and his wife were associate members of the Evangelical Covenant Church of Evanston, Ill. At present they are members at the College Mennonite Church in Goshen, Ind.

He has always had an interest in different religions and churches. During his seminary days he visited Jewish synagogues, Mormon, Christian Science, Bahai, and Buddhist houses of worship, and Unitarian, Catholic, Episcopal, A.M.E., and various Protestant churches. Though he is a layman, he quite frequently gets involved in speaking engagements in churches, non-Mennonite as well as Mennonite.

He remains committed to the believer's church. His interest in comparative religion and ecumenism rises out of and reinforces that commitment. His concern for church discipline reflects this commitment, but it is tested and refined in exposure to and dialogue with other traditions.

Marlin is married to the former Charmaine Shidler of Denver, Colo. They have three children, Eric, Margaret, and David.